T0095306

An Introduction to Christianity

A first-millennium foundation
for third-millennium
thinkers

by
Samuel R. Todd, Jr.

iUniverse, Inc.
Bloomington

AN INTRODUCTION TO CHRISTIANITY
A first-millennium foundation for third-millennium thinkers

iUniverse books may be ordered through booksellers or by contacting:

iUniverse
1663 Liberty Drive
Bloomington, IN 47403
www.iuniverse.com
1-800-Authors (1-800-288-4677)

Because of the dynamic nature of the Internet, any web addresses or links contained in this book may have changed since publication and may no longer be valid. The views expressed in this work are solely those of the author and do not necessarily reflect the views of the publisher, and the publisher hereby disclaims any responsibility for them.

Any people depicted in stock imagery provided by Thinkstock are models, and such images are being used for illustrative purposes only.
Certain stock imagery © Thinkstock.

ISBN: 978-1-4697-7396-4 (sc)
ISBN: 978-1-4697-7397-1 (ebk)

Library of Congress Control Number: 2012911388

Printed in the United States of America

iUniverse rev. date: 02/07/2013

Cover design by Leo Fortuno

For my children
Sam, Peter, Elisa and Miranda
and my godchildren
David Cathcart, Ann Hatchett, Stayton Gammon,
Todd Hutchins and Kevin Ashmore

Preface

An Invitation to the Reader

This book is a product of my pilgrimage into the Christian faith. It is addressed especially to those who are new to it or outside it. The book raises questions I myself have asked over and over, questions like

Is there a God?
How do you know?
Who is man?
What is the point of life?
Hasn't modern science disproved the Bible?
If God is good, why is there so much suffering in the world?
What's so special about Jesus?
Why do I feel lonely when I have so many friends?
What does it mean to be a Christian?
Why is the Church so full of hypocrites?
How can I love my neighbors when I don't even like them?
What happens to us when we die?
What happens to all the good people
    who are not Christian?

The book also gives the answers I have found along the way.

You will find some science, some philosophy, some poetry and theology in this book. I am sure that not all of it will be useful. I hope that some of it will be.

I have written from within the perspective of Anglicanism, a style of Christianity that emerged in the British Isles during the sixteenth and seventeenth centuries when Catholics and Protestants were cutting each other up with swords on the Continent and mainly with words in Britain. Anglicanism sought to discern and maintain a middle way, "not as a compromise for the sake of peace but as a comprehension for the sake of truth."[1] Not all Anglicans, let alone all Christians, would agree with everything I have written. On the other hand, I have written nothing contrary to historic orthodox belief.

The purpose of this book is not to argue you into accepting Christian doctrine but to invite you to share the Christian vision of life and way of life. It has proven to be the way to life for many of us.

Sam Todd

Acknowledgments

I have been blessed with wonderful teachers. Those who had the most influence on me were Merrill Hutchins at St. Stephen's Episcopal School in Austin, Texas; Paul Tillich at Harvard College; Abraham Heschel, John Knox, John Macquarrie and Cyril Richardson at Union Theological Seminary in New York City.

I wish also to thank those who made this book possible. The Episcopal Church of Reconciliation in San Antonio, Texas, gave me the sabbatical in the summer of 1987 during which I wrote the manuscript on a typewriter. Donna Charette typed it onto a computer. Jane Lancaster Patterson did the initial copyediting. She, together with Kip Ashmore, Elizabeth Cauthorn, Jim Crosby, Doug Earle, Mary Earle, Terry Goddard, Bill Green, Walter Herbert, Bob Hibbs, Marie Jones, John Kiel, Bob Sohn, David Stringer and Bettye Wells, read it and gave me encouragement and helpful suggestions. Later Earl Vanzant helped with the formatting, and Evelyn Nolen did exhaustive proofreading and correction of both the first and second editions. Recently Mary Lenn Dixon has been almost solely responsible for editing and getting out this third edition. My debt to all of them is great. The errors and misjudgments that remain are mine.

Contents

I. Knowledge 11

A. How Do We Know? 11
  1) ANYTHING
    (a) Sense Perception
    (b) Reason
    (c) Intuition
    (d) Revelation
    (e) Authority
  2) GOD
    (a) Sense Perception
    (b) Reason
    (c) Intuition
    (d) Revelation
    (e) Authority

B. How Do We Know That We Know?
22
  1) LIMITS
    (a) Sense Perception
    (b) Reason
    (c) Intuition
    (d) Revelation
    (e) Authority
  2) BELIEF
  3) EXPERIENCE

C. Faith 29
  1) AS BELIEF
  2) AS COMMITMENT
  3) AS FIDELITY
  4) AS KNOWLEDGE

D. Samantha's Story...................... 33

II. God 40

A. Toward a Definition.................... 40
  1) WHAT IS AT STAKE
    (a) Love
    (b) Goodness
    (c) Meaning
  2) A PRELIMINARY DEFINITION

B. The Trinity 47
  1) GOD THE FATHER
  2) GOD THE SON
  3) GOD THE HOLY SPIRIT
  4) ONE GOD

C. The Personality of God 54
  1) GRACIOUS
  2) PROVIDENTIAL
  3) POWERFUL

III. Creation 63

A. Substance 65
  1) MATTER
    (a) Energy of the spirit
    (b) Force of love
  2) FORM

B. Finitude 74
  1) LIMITS
    (a) Natural Law
    (b) Matter Is Breakable
    (c) Things Take Time
  2) GOODNESS
  3) MORALITY

C. The Creation as Grace 79
  1) GRACE
    (a) Meaning
    (b) Response
    (c) Original Grace
  2) STEWARDSHIP
    (a) Gratitude
    (b) Property
    (c) Economic Ethics
  3) SACRAMENT
    (a) Meaning
    (b) Creation
    (c) Idolatry

D. A Song of Creation 86

IV. Man 89

A. Creature 89
  1) FINITUDE
  2) HUMILITY

B. Image 93
  1) THE NAKED APE FALLACY
  2) IMAGO DEI
  3) HUMAN NATURE
    (a) Virtue
      i. —Man Is Creative
      ii. —Man Is Social
      iii. —Man Is Free
    (b) Natural Law
    (c) Righteousness

C. Sin 105
  1) FALL
    (a) Pride
    (b) Decadence
    (c) Concupiscence
  2) ORIGINAL SIN
  3) ACTUAL SIN
    (a) The Terror of Human Freedom
    (b) The Power of Sin
    (c) Why Doesn't God . . . ?

V. Christ 115

A. Incarnates God's Love 115
  1) GOD'S PURPOSE
  2) OUR NEED
  3) JESUS CHRIST

B. Teaches God's Love 122
  1) GOD'S LOVE
    (a) The Good News
    (b) The Loving Father
    (c) Our response
  2) LOVE OF NEIGHBOR
    (a) Mercy
    (b) Forgiveness
  3) THE GREAT EQUIVALENCE

C. Ministers God's Love 138
  1) CONFLICT WITH SATAN
    (a) Exorcising Demons
    (b) Healing the Sick
    (c) Forgiving the Sinful
  2) CONFLICT WITH THE
     PHARISEES
  3) CONFLICT WITH ROME

D. The New Creation 155

VI. Church 159

A. Life in the Spirit 160
  1) THE HOLY SPIRIT
    (a) The Content of Grace
    (b) Living from Grace: Paul
       i. —Paul, the Converted
          Pharisee
       ii. —Paul, the Forgiven Sinner
       iii. —Paul, the Inspired Saint
    (c) Discipleship
  2) THE BODY OF CHRIST
    (a) Salvation Is Corporate, Not
        Individual
    (b) The Church Is the Community,
        Not the Building
    (c) It Is Christ's Church, Not Ours
  3) THE HOLY CATHOLIC
     CHURCH
    (a) Her Hypocrisy
    (b) Her Fidelity
    (c) God's Fidelity

B. The Movement into God 178
  1) WORSHIP
  2) THE SACRAMENTS
    (a) Embodiments of Grace
    (b) At Christ's Command
       i. —Baptism
       ii. —The Holy Eucharist
    (c) Other Sacramental Rites
       i. —Confirmation
       ii. —Marriage
       iii. —Reconciliation
       iv. —Unction
       v. —Holy Orders
  3) SPIRITUALITY

C. The Movement into the World .. 192
  1) EVANGELISM
  2) THE WORKS OF MERCY
  3) HEALING SOCIETY
    (a) Church and State
    (b) Justice
    (c) Mercy

VII. Hope................202

A. The End of the World 202
   1) THERE WILL BE AN END
   2) DO NOT ANTICIPATE THE END
   3) LIFT UP YOUR HEADS

B. Heaven and Hell...................... 208
   1) WHAT HAPPENS TO US WHEN
      WE DIE?
   2) WHAT HAPPENS TO
      NON-CHRISTIANS?
   3) WHAT HAPPENS TO THE
      WICKED?

C. The Christian Vision of Life 223

D. A Song of Celebration 231

NOTES 232

INDEX TO BIBLICAL
     REFERENCES 239

INDEX TO KEYWORDS............... 245

ENDORSEMENTS 253

I. Knowledge

How Do We Know?

ANYTHING

When I was seven years old I discovered that Santa Claus did not exist. Soon thereafter I discovered that there was no Easter Bunny. These discoveries immediately raised the question, Is there a God? My parents assured me that, unlike Santa Claus and the Easter Bunny, God really did exist. "But, how do you know?" I asked. Pursuit of this question eventually led me into the study of philosophy and to the more fundamental question, How do you know anything at

I. KNOWLEDGE
A. How Do We Know?
  1) ANYTHING
    (a) Sense Perception
    (b) Reason
    (c) Intuition
    (d) Revelation
    (e) Authority
  2) GOD
    (a) Sense Perception
    (b) Reason
    (c) Intuition
    (d) Revelation
    (e) Authority
B. How Do We Know That We Know?
  1) LIMITS
    (a) Sense Perception
    (b) Reason
    (c) Intuition
    (d) Revelation
    (e) Authority
  2) BELIEF
  3) EXPERIENCE
C. Faith
  1) AS BELIEF
  2) AS COMMITMENT
  3) AS FIDELITY
  4) AS KNOWLEDGE
D. Samantha's Story

all? It is probably impossible to sort out accurately all the ways we acquire knowledge, but surely the main ones are as follows.

Sense Perception

For most of us, seeing is believing. "How do you know it was this man who robbed the bank?" "I saw it with my own eyes." That settles it. "How do you know he called me a jerk?"

"I heard him with my own ears." If I saw it with my own eyes or heard it with my own ears then I know it. The physical senses of sight, hearing, taste, touch, and smell provide the raw data of our experience of external reality, but they do not make sense of the experience.

Reason

Reason is the sense-making part of us. In the broadest sense of the word, reason is the structure of reality and the corresponding structure of the human mind that enables us to apprehend the structure of reality. In the narrow sense of the word, reason is our ability to think accurately either deductively, from the general to the particular, or inductively, from the particular to the general. An example of the former is the syllogism: All men are animals; John is a man; therefore John is an animal. An example of the later would be a research project that observes that John, Dick, Harry and 997 other men have two arms and concludes that all men do. The modern scientific method of apprehending reality is mainly a combination of sensation and reason. Data are collected by careful observation and measurement. An hypothesis is formulated that will subsume the data under some helpful generalization, for example, a body at rest or in motion will remain at rest or in motion in a straight line unless acted upon by an outside force. The hypothesis is then tested by repeated experiment and if confirmed becomes a theory or even a descriptive law of nature. Newton's law of inertia, just mentioned, came about this way. The scientific method works beautifully for those aspects of reality that are repetitive such as the rotation of the earth and quantifiable like height, weight, and velocity. I say that the scientific method is mainly a combination of sensation and reason because the hypothesis itself is often the result of neither observation nor reasoning but of intuition.

Intuition

Intuition is immediate knowledge. I have intuitive knowledge of myself; I do not have to see myself in a mirror or go through a process of reasoning to know that I am. Space, time, causality, and substance are neither observed nor inferred but are intuitive categories in terms of which we experience and reason about reality. Intuition is an elusive dynamic within the orderly method of scientific progress. A genius will have an intuitive hypothesis proven true by experiment but not preceded by inference. Its effect will be a breakthrough; its origin will remain unaccountable even to the genius himself. It has come to him like a revelation.

Revelation

In Spanish there are two words for knowledge—*saber*, knowledge of facts, and *conocer*, acquaintance with persons. Saber is knowledge about a person: his name, date of birth, height, weight and other "vital statistics." To know these things is not to know the person himself. I can see his physical appearance and make inferences from his actions about his character; I cannot know his heart and mind from the outside. Conocer knowledge may be had only in personal relationship;

it is a gift that may be received but not possessed. A man's soul is expressed in his thoughts and feelings, and these I may know only if he reveals them to me through his word and spirit. A person's spirit is not just the principle of his vitality but the expression of his soul. I may be of a gentle spirit or a humble spirit or a troubled spirit. My spirit will make an impression on you, but I can reveal the inmost workings of my mind best through my words. You can know me only as I become open to revealing myself to you; conversely, I will be open to revealing myself to the extent I sense your being open to receive me. In other words, revelation usually occurs in a context of love. The important gift of revelation is not saber but conocer, not information but a relationship.

Authority

Most of what we know is not from our own knowledge but what we learn from authority. We have taken someone's word for it, someone who knows what he is talking about, that is, an authority. If I based my belief only on what I see, I would think the sun revolves around the earth, but I accept the astronomer's word for it that the earth actually revolves around the sun. All past events, all events that happen outside the narrow compass of my sight, I know of only because a historian or reporter tells me. I do not have direct knowledge of when Julius Caesar lived or even that he lived; I have read about him in the history books. The world looks solid to me; I accept the physicist's word that it actually is composed of molecules composed of atoms, which are mainly empty space.

Authority makes growth in knowledge possible. We are able to invent computers because we do not have to reinvent the wheel. Newton said that he had seen farther than other men because he had stood on the shoulders of giants;[1] he is one of the giants upon whose shoulders we stand.

GOD

We know God in roughly the same way that we know anything else.

Sense Perception

This is the exception. Many of us are looking for God, but we will never find him with our physical sight or hear him with our ears. He is invisible, intangible, inaudible. At the end of a cloudy night I once sat waiting for the sunrise. Slowly, gradually the sky lightened, the trees, bushes, and grass around me became visible, but the sun itself never appeared. God is like that. In his light we see; him we do not see. His handiwork is all around us, is us, but the hand is invisible. We track his footprints but never find the feet. Some of our brightest scientists spend their lives unraveling the clues of the creation; the mystery of the Creator cannot be unraveled.

Reason

The creation does contain clues, and the greatest of them is the fact of the creation itself. Why should there be something instead of nothing? We awake each morning to a self we did not create in a body we did not create to a world we did not create.

Who did? Every creature we know was brought into being by something else that was caused by something else that was caused by something else. Without an uncaused first cause, that is, a Creator, the chain of causation would never have begun. Every reality we know is temporary; there was a time when it was not. The law of conservation of mass/energy tells us that nothing comes from nothing. We do not have "to be"; we do not have being as a possession, but rather as a donation. Whose? Without an ultimate, original, necessary, eternal reality who is to be and who gives reality to all contingent, temporal reality, there would be no reality at all. We know that mass can be converted to energy and vice versa. Einstein figured out the equivalence: $E=mc^2$. The amount of energy released will be equal to the amount of mass multiplied by the square of the velocity of light (i.e., 186,326 x 186,326 miles per second). So an enormous amount of energy is contained in a small amount of mass; 1/28th of an ounce of mass, totally converted to energy will produce the energy released in the Hiroshima explosion.[2] To turn that around, $m=E/c^2$. In other words, it took an enormous amount of energy to produce the creation. Whose energy? Not mine certainly. Not yours either.

But suppose that ultimate reality is just something like hydrogen gas and that all other reality has evolved from just chance collisions and concatenations of particles, atoms, molecules and so forth? It seems unlikely on the face of it. If I take the back off a watch and see the intricate arrangement of its parts all working together it seems reasonable to assume that someone designed it and did so for a purpose.[3] Nature is much more complex than a watch. We humans can make a watch; we cannot make so much as a mouse. "Mouse is miracle enough"[4] to point human reason to a divine intelligence. Charles Townes, who holds the Noble Prize for developing the laser, has called our attention to the Antropic Principle: "What this means is that complex, carbon-based life—namely, us—can exist only in a universe tuned just so. Take the ratio of gravity to electromagnetism. If gravity were a tiny bit stronger, we'd be pulled apart; if electromagnetism were a tiny bit stronger, we'd fall in on ourselves like failed souffles." "We do not know why the physical constants are what they are," Mr. Townes noted, "but many have a feeling that somehow intelligence must have been involved in the laws of the universe."[5] Someone has said that it is as likely our present universe came about purely by chance as that a monkey randomly hitting the keys of a typewriter would type out the complete works of Shakespeare. Someone else has said that the monkey could do it given an infinite amount of time. But there has not been an infinite amount of time; the universe has only been around for about fifteen billion years and the earth for only about five billion. What would the monkey's chances be? On my typewriter there are forty-four keys containing eighty-eight characters, plus a space bar. That is not counting the shift key. In order for the monkey to type the complete works of Shakespeare he would first have to type out, by chance, the word *The*. His chance of hitting a capital *T* is 1 in 89; his chance of hitting a lower case *h* is also 1 in 89 as is his chance of hitting a lower case *e* and the space bar. But his chance of hitting these four keys in the exact sequence is 1 in 89 times 89 times 89 times 89. In my edition of the complete works of Shakespeare there are at least five letters in the average word, 640 words to the page and 1528 pages. In other words, there are approximately 4,889,600 letters in the Shakespearean corpus. The chances of a monkey randomly typing that are 1 in 89 multiplied by 89—4,889,600 times. Simply to write that number out would take more pages than are in this book. This universe came about by chance? Not very likely.

But if the universe evolved purposefully, why does not science say so? Because the scientific method is unequipped to detect purpose. Science observes the what of creation and can untangle the how of it but has no clue as to the why of it. Science cannot even detect my purposes. It can observe my actions and explain the mechanics of them but not why I do them. My purposes are revealed only through my words.

Intuition

Humans have always known there was God and were religious before they were human, or at least Homo Sapiens. Neanderthal burial practices bespeak their religious sense. The history of religions and the study of primitive religion make clear that religion did not begin as primitive science but as primitive mysticism, not as an attempt to explain how the trees grow, the stars twinkle and the sun shines, but as awe, wonder, reverence for and a sense of kinship with the power of life that was all around and beyond them. Religion begins with intuition, immediate awareness of the numinous, experience of the Holy, encounter with the Other. Then people tell stories, ransacking human language for symbols and metaphors to try to communicate their experience and its implications for their lives. Then the intellectuals of the religious community reflect upon the experiences and stories and try to make rational, self-consistent and systematic sense of them and to integrate religious knowledge with all other human knowledge. In other words, first comes religious experience, then story, then theology.

From the beginning then, people "were to seek God, and it might be, touch and find him; though indeed he is not far from each one of us, for in him we live and move, in him we exist" (Acts 17:27f). As if he were the ocean and we fish within it, "in him we live and move, in him we exist." As if he were the air and we birds, "in him we live and move, in him we exist."

Can we relate to God today? We cannot help but be related to him any more than any of us can avoid having a relationship with the air. The air is all around us and within us; it permeates the room in which we sit though it is invisible and we are rarely aware of its presence. We would be acutely aware of its absence; for, though we ignore it, are ignorant of it, we breathe it in at every moment. In it we live and move; in it and by it we exist. The problem is simply lack of awareness. I used to scoff at how stupid primitive people were for relating to trees as if they were alive; then I realized that trees are alive. It is only my insensitivity and ignorance that causes me to regard them as mere things, objects to be walked around instead of being aware of them as living beings.

Revelation

The word *revelation* means to remove the veil; it points to the divine, self-disclosing, side of religious experience. What is disclosed in revelation is not information about God or the world, but God himself. The knowledge that comes from revelation is *conocer* not *saber*. Reason will lead us to the conclusion that God is, but only by means of revelation do we become acquainted with who God is. God expresses and discloses himself through the Word, who structures creation, reveals the mind of God to the prophets, and becomes incarnate in Jesus Christ. God expresses and discloses himself through the Spirit who energizes creation, inspires the prophets, and animates the Church.

Authority

Though the word *revelation* can be used to indicate any self-disclosure of divine being, including that mediated through the creation, the word is more narrowly, and perhaps properly, reserved for that special mode of religious experience in which decisive and formative insights into who God is are granted, like those given to Moses and Jesus. Revelation, in the proper sense of the word, is a rare occurrence; I have never received any and do not expect to. God, as author of being, is of course the ultimate authority. But people like Moses and Jesus become authorities, too, in the sense that they are acknowledged to know what they are talking about because they are well acquainted with God. Religious communities grow up around such people and their teaching. The teaching is lived out in and by the community and is existentially validated and amplified in the life of the community, especially in the lives of the prophets, apostles, martyrs and saints. Being part of a community of faith saves me from having to start from scratch in my knowledge of God. And the experience of the community over the centuries guides and corrects my own experience of God and the ideas about him that flow from that experience. I was not privileged to stand on Mt. Sinai. I did not get to walk the Galilean hills with Jesus, but some people did and their story has come down to us. They tell us: "It was there from the beginning; we have heard it; we have seen it with our own eyes; we looked upon it, and felt it with our own hands; and it is of this we tell. Our theme is the word of life. This life was made visible; we have seen it and bear our testimony" (I St. Jn. 1:1–2). I accept their testimony; I accept the disciples as an authority, that is, that they know what they are talking about because they were there.

The disciples' letters and Gospels are contained in the Bible, a collection of books the Church has written and considers authoritative because the particular people who wrote them were intimately connected with the revelatory events described. A record of our fathers' encounters with the Holy, the Bible has become itself holy and can be a means of our encounter with the Holy One. The Bible informs and constrains all subsequent Church teaching about God; it is the Church's foundational document somewhat similar to the American Constitution in function. Though the Bible's chief concern is to recount the evolving relationship between God and his community, it also contains explicitly or by implication history, political theory, love poetry, and primitive science. For example the Bible assumes the earth is flat. Obviously the ancient science contained in the Bible is obsolete. It would be silly to do bad science and call it faith. It is in its religious teaching that the Bible is authoritative.

So, the ways we know about God and even know God himself are not too different from the ways we know anything else.

How Do We Know That We Know?

LIMITS

To err is human. To make mistakes in knowledge as well as in behavior is a common experience. How can we be sure, how can we be absolutely certain that we know what we think we know? The problem is not subjective certitude, for many people have felt certain, have been convinced beyond the shadow of a doubt, of something that turned out not to be true. The problem is objective certitude. Does human knowledge admit of objective certitude? Is human knowledge of such a character that proof positive may be had? To make a long story short, the answer is no.

Sense Perception

Sense perception, which gives us our raw data about the world, is the product of a relationship between the knower and the known, the viewer and the viewed. Each contributes something to the experience and it is finally impossible to disentangle how much is contributed by the perceiving subject and how much by the perceived object. The wall in front of me would look very different if I were on LSD. What makes me think that I see it accurately now? It would look different if I were color blind. As it is, the range of my perception is narrow, for I see reality only as illumined by that narrow band of the electromagnetic radiation spectrum we call visible light. How much richer reality would look if I could see it as illumined with radio waves, X rays, cosmic rays, infrared or ultraviolet radiation! What would the world sound like if my range of hearing were twice what it is? A stick stuck in the water looks bent; my eyes have deceived me. What makes us think that reality is as it appears to be? No matter how sophisticated we make microscopes and telescopes and other extensions of our sensation, the range of our perception is always limited. Moreover, and more importantly, what we are perceiving is not necessarily the thing itself but the thing as it appears to us.[6] There is finally, by definition, no way of knowing what reality is apart from the way it appears to us. Thus strictly speaking, what modern science is busily observing, categorizing, and theorizing about are phenomena, appearances that may or may not correspond to the reality beneath the appearances.

Reason

Some things seem reasonable that turn out not to be true. If event B invariably follows event A, it seems reasonable to conclude that event B is caused by event A. A rooster named

Chanticleer[7] was very proud of making the sun rise. He knew he did because every morning he would crow and shortly thereafter, invariably, the sun rose. It is interesting to note that causation itself is an assumption; we never actually see anything cause anything else; all we see is a succession of events. The rooster's reasoning is known as the post hoc ergo propter hoc (after that, therefore because that) fallacy.

Mathematics and deductive reasoning are certain. Math is certain for the same reason chess is. I know for sure that 2+2=4, for the same reason I know for sure that, if my king is in check and I can neither capture the attacking piece nor move my king nor interpose a piece between my king and the attacker, then I am checkmated. I know this for certain because both mathematics and chess are games of human invention and all the terms and rules are of human invention. Unfortunately neither math nor chess nor deductive logic gives us information about the outside world. If Paris is in France and France is in Asia then I know for certain that Paris is in Asia. The logic is impeccable but the conclusion is false because one of the premises is false and logic cannot supply the premises.

Inductive reasoning is always uncertain. Even if all one thousand men I study have two arms it is still hazardous for me to conclude that all men do. And in fact of course not all do. Inductive reasoning produces probabilities not certainties, the greater the survey sample, the greater the probability (presumably).

Reasoning about God yields no more proof than reasoning about reality in general. St. Anselm said God is that than which nothing greater can be conceived. Either he exists or he does not exist. If he does not exist then we can conceive of something greater than God, namely a God who does exist. But conceiving of something greater than God is logically absurd. Therefore the alternative must be true, namely that God exists.[8] The reasoning is fine, but the proof assumes a complete identity between the order of reason and the order of reality, and this identity cannot be proven.

As improbable as it seems, perhaps the monkey could type out the complete works of Shakespeare by pure chance. Perhaps the astounding, intricate, interlocked order of the universe is, after all, an accident, a randomly arrived at happy happenstance.

Intuition

"They asked me how I knew my true love was true. I of course replied, 'Something here inside cannot be denied.'"[9] Poor fellow; his intuition misled him; smoke got in his eyes. The problem with intuitions about God or anything else is that I can never be certain they are not just my liver acting up, that I am not producing the perception. I am aware of being surrounded by being and of being sustained in being from moment to moment. But how can I be aware that that being has an infinite source and support?

Revelation

The problem with ordinary revelations is that the person revealing his mind to me through his words may be lying.

Leaving aside the possibility of God lying to us, the problem with divine revelation is that man conditions it with his own finitude in the act of receiving it. God may be infinite, but we are not; he may be infallible, but we are not; he may be beyond the vicissitudes of history and culture, but we are not. All revelation is conditioned by the cultural context and personal makeup of the people who receive it. Did God really tell Samuel to tell Saul to make a holocaust of the Amalekites, to slaughter them man, woman and child? (I Sam. 15:2–3) I do not think so; I hope not.

Authority

By whose authority is the authority an authority? The history of the progress of human knowledge is a story of the experts being proved wrong. It is also a story of the overturning of received wisdom and common sense. In practice we accept as authoritative what our culture tells us. For example we do not experience many miracles nowadays partly because the culture tells us they cannot happen. In fact, science only describes what does happen; it does not say what can and cannot happen. But if I have an experience totally contrary to my expectations, I am as likely to doubt that I had the experience as I am to change my expectations. Authority is hard to overturn; it is also not an infallible guide.

The authority issue has caused more dissension in religious communities than has any other issue. Revelation to one person, when he reports it to others, is, to them, simply a report of revelation and an implicit claim to authority. And the problem of false prophets is as old as prophecy. A first-century Christian document called The Teaching of the Twelve Apostles says

> Let every apostle who comes to you be received as the Lord. But he shall not remain more than one day. . . . If he stays for three he is a false prophet. And when the apostle departs, let him take only enough bread to last until he reaches shelter; but, if he asks for money, he is a false prophet. And you shall not tempt any prophet who speaks in the spirit, or judge him; for every sin shall be forgiven, but this sin shall not be forgiven. But not everyone who speaks in the spirit is a prophet, but only if he follows the conduct of the Lord. Accordingly, from their conduct the false prophet and the true prophet will be known. No prophet who in the spirit orders a meal to be prepared eats from it; but, if he does, he is a false prophet.[10]

One advantage that members of the "institutional Church" have over the audiences of television evangelists is that the Church learned a long time ago how to guard against profit-making prophets. But, a chronicle of statements by religious authorities of the institutional Church that are embarrassing to their present-day followers would make for lengthy reading. It is easy enough to say that God himself is the ultimate religious authority; the problem is how his authority is communicated to us. It is surely a mistake to invest anything less than God, whether it be the Bible or the pope, with absolute religious authority.

I am not saying that we cannot have genuine knowledge of reality or of God, only that we cannot be certain that we do.

All knowledge, secular and religious, is gained by methods the infallibility of which cannot be demonstrated.

BELIEF

All knowledge, secular and religious, is ultimately based upon belief. The basic belief of science is that there is an order underlying apparently disconnected and random physical events, that, as Einstein said, "God does not play dice."[11] More specifically, the scientist believes that the Copernican model of the solar system is a more helpful way of accounting for observed celestial phenomena than is the Ptolemaic model and quantum mechanics is a more useful model than classical Newtonian mechanics in accounting for sub-atomic phenomena. The historian believes that this set of records is useful in reconstructing past events. The psychoanalyst believes that Freudian categories like ego, superego, and id are a therapeutically helpful model of psychological phenomena. The Christian believes that God is who Jesus Christ said he is.

EXPERIENCE

The beliefs that underlie contemporary scientific, historical, psychological and religious knowledge are not ultimately provable. But neither are they arbitrary. No one just sat down and made them up out of whole cloth. They have evolved out of human experience with reality; they are constantly tested against our experience of reality and are maintained because they are found useful in understanding (making sense out of) and relating to reality, including ultimate reality. Of course some ways of understanding nature—quantification, for example—are not helpful in understanding God. And some ways of relating to nature are inappropriate in relating to God. It is possible to subdue and manipulate some of nature to our own ends; we call that technology. The attempt to do the same thing with God is called magic, and it does not work. The Bible and the subsequent history, spirituality and theology of the Christian Church are products of a particular religious community's four thousand years' experience of living with God. The beliefs we hold today and our teachings (doctrine) about them are those we have found helpful in relating to God and in understanding and improving human life. Pragmatism—what works best over the long haul—is the actual acid test of all knowledge, secular and religious.

Faith

I would like to know for sure, and I would like for my life to be risk-free. But those are not possible. I must live from faith or live, less boldly, from lack of it. What is faith? The word has several levels of meaning.

AS BELIEF

The word *belief* can mean mere opinion. "Is the plane due to arrive at six o'clock?" "I don't know but I believe so." "What is the capital of Mongolia?" "I believe it is Ulan Bator." "Will it rain?" "I believe so." One can say "I believe that God exists" in just the same way. That is not speaking in faith but simply stating a theological opinion. But whether we believe in God or do not believe in God makes no difference to God so long as our belief is just opinion. If the Bible is to be believed, our opinions cut no ice with God because they cut no ice with us. If our opinions make no difference in our lives, they are religiously worthless.

Yet belief is the most frequent demand Jesus puts upon his hearers in the Gospel of John. "Set your troubled hearts at rest. Ye believe in God; believe also in me" (John 14:1 KJV). This is belief in rather than belief that; it is trust not opinion. Notice the New English Bible's translation: "Set your troubled hearts at rest. Trust in God always; trust also in me." Trust is the willingness to act upon belief, and it involves risk. Faith is the kind of belief a paratrooper has in his parachute. He cannot know for certain that it will open, but he is willing to stake his life on his belief that it will. Faith is jumping out of the airplane. I believe in my surgeon's competence, my banker's honesty, my wife's fidelity. These beliefs have the character of faith because I have something at stake.

AS COMMITMENT

The reason that belief is crucial to faith is that without it one never embarks on the life of faith within which alone faith can be validated. When Jesus says, "Believe in me," he is saying "Follow me." The nice thing about philosophers like Socrates and scientists like Newton is that when they say, "The unexamined life is not worth living" or "For every action there is an equal and opposite reaction," one does not need to know anything about them personally to find out whether their statements are true. And having validated their statements, we have no further need of them. Not so with Jesus. When he says, "I am the way, the truth and the life" (Jn. 14:6) or "I am the resurrection and I am life. If a man has faith in me, even though he die, he shall come to life; and no one who is alive and has faith shall ever die. Do you believe this?" (Jn. 11:25ff), the truth of his statements entirely depends on who he is, and I cannot find out except by following him. The Christian faith can never be validated, or even really understood, from the outside. It can only be validated from the inside, as a player not as a spectator. We have evidence enough for courage, not enough to make the venture unnecessary. Fundamentalism is less, not more, faithful than traditional orthodox belief because, in addition to making the Bible into an idol, it tries to take the risk out of faith. If there were no doubt, I would not need faith.

AS FIDELITY

The Marine Corps motto is Semper Fidelis (Always Faithful). What is meant by *faithful* is reliable, dependable. When we need them, the Marines will be there. When the going gets rough, they will still be there. Fidelity is keeping faith with someone. It is the kind of faith God promises his people; it is the meaning of the Hebrew word *hesed*. It is the kind of faith Job averred, "Though he slay me, yet will I trust in him" (Job 3:15 KJV). It is the kind of faith God showed us in Christ, whom we did slay. It is the kind of faith Peter promised but did not at first deliver: "Everyone else may fall away on your account but I never will. . . . Even if I must die with you, I will never disown you" (Mt. 26:33, 35). This is the faith displayed by the martyrs. Fidelity is ultimately the meaning of discipleship. Christian faith is keeping faith with Christ day in and day out, year in and year out, even when I am not getting any joy, peace, enlightenment or consolation out of it. The man who says his business has doubled since he gave his life to Christ is not making a witness of faith, but of successfully calculated self-interest. Here is a faith witness: "I count everything sheer loss, because all is far outweighed by the gain of knowing Christ Jesus my Lord, for whose sake I did in fact lose everything. I count it so much dung, for the sake of gaining Christ and finding myself incorporate in him . . ." (Phil. 3:8f).

AS KNOWLEDGE

Though we have faith in lieu of knowledge, paradoxically, faith gives us a knowledge of its own. When a football player says before a game, or a soldier before a battle, "I know we will win," he is speaking from the knowledge of faith. In one sense of course he cannot know since the game is yet to be played, the battle to be fought. And yet he knows already, and his knowledge helps to bring about the result he already knows. This causative quality is a peculiar characteristic of the knowledge of faith. How often Jesus tells someone he has healed, "Thy faith hath made thee whole."

Faith gives knowledge in a second sense too. It is *conocer* knowledge, acquaintance with God, which we cannot obtain except by embarking upon the life of faith. One is a fool to marry someone he does not know. One is also a fool to think he knows the person he is marrying. I know my wife now in a depth and breadth that would have been impossible to obtain except by living with her for many years in the covenant of marriage. We gain the same sort of knowledge of God by having enough faith in him to risk living with him faithfully. It does not make us great theologians, but it gives us a pretty good feel for his character.

Job spoke from both these senses of the knowledge of faith when he said: "I know that my Redeemer liveth, and that he shall stand at the latter day upon the earth; and though this body be destroyed, yet shall I see God; whom I shall see for myself and mine eyes shall behold, and not as a stranger."[12]

Samantha's Story

Samantha was a bright girl and increasingly well educated, except theologically. She became a Sunday School dropout at age twelve after she was confirmed in a burst of prepubescent faith. She took into her adolescence an image of God as a magical man in the sky who looked over her, who controlled all things, and to whom she could talk in prayer. Her prayer life consisted mostly of tugging at the pants leg of the magical man in the sky saying, "Dear Lord, gimme this and I want that and please make this thing happen and don't let this other thing take place." Samantha assumed that the magical man in the sky existed mainly for the purpose of advancing her own selfishness. But the magical man in the sky granted few of the favors Samantha asked; so, she prayed less and less and eventually stopped altogether.

Samantha began studying science in high school and learned enough of it to be impressed by the regularity of nature and to be awed by the simplicity and dependability of nature's laws. She did not yet know enough of science to know that its laws are descriptive not prescriptive, telling what is done not what can be, describing only the routine, incapable of dealing with the unique and immeasurable.

She also studied world religions and found that people have had many different notions of God. This discovery eroded her image of God and, since she knew nothing else of God, it eroded her faith in God himself. Seeing many images, she concluded that none could be correct and, further, that that of which they were images was nothing; for, she could not imagine an ineffable, imageless reality. So she bade good-bye to God as a childish superstition.

Not that the leave-taking was sad. No need had she of bogey men and witch doctors and superstitious talk. The world and life lay before her as prizes to be conquered and comprehended. She rejoiced when she discovered and could repeat LaPlace's dictum about God: "I have no need of that hypothesis."[13] She had the unconscious self-confidence of youth—that her destiny was in her own hands and that nothing was incomprehensible. She assumed that anything she could not understand must not exist.

Samantha went to a progressive high school that offered many electives. In her senior year she took biology, astronomy and paleontology. That is when the trouble began. One day she looked through a microscope at a drop of water, not for the first time of course. But while she was gazing at the myriad of minute organisms swimming around, she was suddenly struck with the realization that there is a whole other world down there where inches are miles and each droplet a nation teaming with life. And within the world of microbes lies the still smaller one of molecules and, within that, worlds of atoms. She grew afraid and wondered that she should be here rather than there. It was then that she went to a psychiatrist to share her fears.

No sooner had she begun her therapy than Samantha looked through a telescope at the heavens. While looking at the hundreds of stars she had never seen with her naked eye, she realized that the telescope was but a larger eye and that beyond its range perhaps lay worlds and stars and galaxies as yet undreamed-of. She grew afraid and wondered that she should be here rather than there.

In her paleontology class she learned of the dinosaurs that had lived 150 million years ago and of the trilobites that had lived 500 million years ago. She began musing that for most of time earth has not existed and that for most of the time the earth has existed, life has not and that for most of the time life has existed, man has not and that for most of the time man has existed, civilization has not and that for most of the time civilization has existed she had not. She had frequently thought the past was irrelevant to her; now she realized she was irrelevant to the past and to the future as well. From time immemorial the world had existed quite nicely without her and, but a short time hence, it would do so once again. She was struck by the ephemerality of her life, which was like that of a south Texas snowflake, which falls through the air for a few brief moments and no sooner strikes the ground than it is gone. Samantha did not know the names of her great grandparents and she knew that her great grandchildren would not remember her either. She went to her psychiatrist and said, "When I consider the infinity of space lying beneath me and the infinity of space lying beyond me, when I consider the infinity of time lying behind me and the infinity of time lying before me, I grow afraid and wonder that I should be here rather than there, now rather than then."[14] Her psychiatrist tried to help Samantha figure out the name of the power that had seized her. Her parents told her she thought too much.

Samantha was a searcher, and in her searching she kept bumping up against the limits of her life. She had dared to peer over the edge of her world and had grown giddy at the vista of worlds within worlds whirling within and without her world. She had journeyed to the edge of her finitude and had confronted the infinite. Long she stood there fearful yet fascinated, wondering what name to give to that mystery that both thrilled and enthralled her.

Like most of us Samantha had a thirst for knowledge of all kinds, but she could never find the knowledge she sought. The more she studied, the less she knew. For example, she entered college certain that the earth revolved around the sun and not vice verse. But she found her teacher unwilling to say that; he would only say that science found the heliocentric model more useful than the geocentric one. "But which is it really?" she asked. "What do you mean by 'really'?" her teacher asked. "If you stood off in space and looked, would you see the earth going around the sun or the sun going around the earth?" she asked. "That would depend on where you stood," the teacher said. "If you stood above the sun, (that is, if you and the sun were two points defining a line perpendicular to the plane of the ecliptic), then you would indeed see the earth revolving around the sun. But if you stood directly above the earth, then what you would see with your very own eyes would be the sun revolving around the earth." This was the first of many instances that showed Samantha that all her knowledge was dependent upon her point of view. And the more she studied she came to realize that her knowledge was small compared to all that there was to know and that what lay outside the scope of her intellect would always far exceed what lay within that tiny compass. She was not sure what to call the power that had set her thirsting for knowledge but rendered her knowing preliminary, tenuous, and relative. But she was in that power's grasp and went back to her psychiatrist to tell him about it.

Samantha hungered for love as most of us do. She wanted her empty places filled, her loneliness dissipated by being with someone else. She was so happy when after many dreary dates she finally fell in love with someone who loved her. But, poor Samantha, she soon discovered a problem: she could never totally be with her lover. In the very act of kissing him she would be aware that she was kissing him and also aware that it was getting close to the hour she had to be back in the dorm.

At the same time she was aware that she was aware of all this and was angry about it. Her ability to be present to her beloved was undermined by the self within the self that is aware of the self and also aware of its self-awareness. How is that self to be engaged, addressed, loved? Samantha became aware that for all her fullness she was unfulfilled, that there was an empty place within the self that her lover could not even reach, let alone fill. Samantha peered down the well at the center of herself and could not see the bottom of it; she sought to plumb the depths of her soul and found them to be abysmal.

Samantha grew in another kind of love as well, that of mercy and compassion. But the more compassionate she became, the more aware she became of all the suffering in the world, and the more she suffered that suffering. The more loving she became, the more pain she felt, and that correlation baffled her. She became overwhelmed by the infinite pathos of life, for which only an infinite pity is sufficient. And Samantha was not infinite, though she was somehow bound to the infinite and permeated by it.

Her psychiatrist could not name the power that had thrust her into life here and now and would cut her off from life shortly, that set her thirsting for knowledge but rendered all her knowing puny and relative, that created depths within her that cried out for love but made them of infinite proportions, which only an infinite love could fill. But gradually Samantha ceased resenting her bondage and her fascination overcame her fear. One night when the lights were out and the familiar forms of the day fallen away, when her roommate was asleep and Samantha left alone, when deep called to deep, the abyss within to the abyss without, Samantha gave voice to her love and said, "My Father, my Father, who art in heaven."

That was the beginning and a long time ago. One of her recent prayers goes like this: "Let only that little be left of me whereby I may name thee my all. Let only that little be left of my will whereby I may feel thee on every side, and come to thee in everything, and offer to thee my love every moment. Let only that little be left of me whereby I may never hide thee. Let only that little of my fetters be left whereby I am bound with thy will and thy purpose is carried out in my life—and that is the fetter of thy love."[15]

II. God

Toward a Definition

II. GOD
A. Toward A Defintion
    1) WHAT IS AT STAKE
        (a) Love
        (b) Goodness
        (c) Meaning
    2) A PRELIMINARY DEFINTION
B. The Trinity
    1) GOD THE FATHER
    2) GOD THE SON
    3) GOD THE HOLY SPIRIT
    4) ONE GOD
C. The Personality of God
    1) GRACIOUS
    2) PROVIDENTIAL
    3) POWERFUL

It is important how one raises the question of God. One could simply define *God* as ultimate reality and then ask after the nature of that reality. The quarry of such a quest will prove to be the "god of the philosophers," that is, Being-Itself, the lowest common denominator and the ultimate abstraction. Is this he who commanded the Hebrews at Mt. Sinai or came to dwell among us at Bethlehem? Whatever deserves the name "God" must be able to command my love and obedience as well as dazzle my mind. If the quest for ultimate reality is reduced to the quest for the ultimate physical substance and the quest confined to modern scientific methods, the quarry may be found to be "Super-Strings."[1] Even less than Being-Itself is this what I had in mind at age seven when I asked "Is there really a God?"

The opposite alternative is to take one's childish image of God and then seek to know whether that image corresponds to anything that can be found within the realm of reality. This quest leads to the answer "No." And anything found within the realm of reality would be one being among others, not ultimate, not worthy of the name "God." So "God" implies ultimacy and sovereignty. Whatever else God is, he cannot be a matter of indifference. At this point, it is appropriate to ask the question directly, "What difference does it make if God is?"

WHAT IS AT STAKE

Love

If there is no God, love is always defeated in the end. Erotic love is defeated. *Eros* is "the desire for the perpetual possession of the good."[2] In loving a woman erotically, I am attracted by her good qualities: her beauty, wit, vitality, integrity, charm, etc. I want to have her, to possess the good, to unite with her. But my desire for union is frustrated by corporeality, sin and death. Milton said that when angels make love they simply flow together, merging their incorporeal beings.[3] But we cannot do that; our bodies are both the instruments and obstacles to union.

People fall back upon romantic love in a despairing age. Matthew Arnold wrote:

The Sea of Faith
Was once, too, at the full, and round earth's shore
Lay like the folds of a bright girdle furled.
But now I only hear
Its melancholy, long, withdrawing roar,
Retreating, to the breath
Of the night-wind, down the vast edges drear
And naked shingles of the world.

Ah, love, let us be true
To one another! for the world, which seems
To lie before us like a land of dreams,
So various, so beautiful, so new,
Hath really neither joy, nor love, nor light,
Nor certitude, nor peace, nor help for pain;
And we are here as on a darkling plain
Swept with confused alarms of struggle and flight,
Where ignorant armies clash by night.[4]

But lovers' fidelity, let alone unity, is eventually frustrated by each one's will-to-power, fear for personal identity, and simple pettiness. The great enemy is death, whose clammy hands rest upon the shoulders of all lovers. Even the rare lovers who survive all the vicissitudes of courtship and marriage end alone. They never die in each other's arms simultaneously. Each dies his own death. One predeceases the other, and the survivor is abandoned. And it is the very best marriages that produce the loneliest widowhood. If there is no God, loneliness, not love, is the last word.

Agape love is also defeated. *Agape*, the New Testament word for love, formerly translated "charity," is to will and act for someone else's best interest. It is love not just because of what is attractive but in spite of what is unattractive in another. It is the love of mercy, forgiveness, and self-sacrifice. Such love is the strongest force in the world because it alone can overcome sin, guilt, and estrangement, converting the enemy into a friend; but it is also the weakest force in the world because it can do nothing except by consent of the beloved and because it does not and cannot resist evil. It is often crucified in this world. Jesus exemplified such love and was killed. Upon that most of us can agree; only Christians believe he was raised from the dead. Without God there is no resurrection, and the highest form of love is the most foolish of follies.

Goodness

If there is no God, there is no ground for goodness or hope for ultimate justice. The logical positivist A. J. Ayer said that all ethical judgments are literally meaningless; they are emotive outbursts not propositions about reality.[5] To say "torture is evil" is equivalent to saying "torture!" in a tone of horror or disgust. All it means is "I don't like it." I do not like rum raisin ice cream either. "Torture is evil" has the same truth value as "rum raisin ice cream, yuck!" Ethics are matters of taste not of truth. Unless God exists, Ayer is right. You and I may put Hitler and St. Francis in very different moral categories, but they are both dead, and the blind eyes of the sun, the moon and the stars see no difference between them. The sun, the moon and the stars do not care if you torture someone. The question is whether the universe is morally blind apart from the finite, flickering moral vision of mankind. Is there an absolute, holy reality whose will is the enduring norm that informs, judges and supersedes all finite groping toward goodness? If not, good and evil are finally meaningless categories. Dostoevsky's Raskolnikov said, "If there is no God, all things are possible."[6] That is a truism of moral nihilism that an increasingly atheistic world is increasingly acting upon.

If justice is the triumph of good over evil, then without God there is no hope for final justice even if we could agree that good is a meaningful category without God. World history is replete with merciless murderers who carved out Empires—Genghis Khan and his Mongols, for example; Adolf Hitler and his Nazis, for a more recent one. Genghis Khan died a natural death; Hitler put a bullet through his head after his policies caused the death of over 25 million people in six years. Does Hitler's easy death compensate for the deaths of 25 million people, many of whom were gentle folk who wished only to be left alone to till their fields but instead were killed, sometimes only after slow ordeals of agony? Leaving aside for the moment whether their deaths should be avenged or what it would mean for them to be redeemed, without God there is no hope for either vengeance or redemption.

Without God there is also no hope for justice in the sense of correction to unfairness. Life is plainly unfair. It is not as unfair as we sometimes think. If I, who smoke, get lung cancer, that is not unfair. If you are lazy and irresponsible and never make your way very far in the world, that is not unfair. If people who are selfish, suspicious and critical die unloved and unmourned, that is not unfair. But much of life is. The single most reliable predictor of worldly success is the accident of birth. Some are born healthy and intelligent; others are born damaged in mind or limb. Some are born rich, others desperately poor. The single greatest secret to making a small fortune is to start with a large fortune. Advancement is sometimes unfair. Patient merit is not always recognized and promoted while many scoundrels and charlatans have risen to the peaks of prestige. Death is almost always unfair. We die too soon or too late and frequently the undeserving survive while the best are cut down before their time. Without God, there is no hope for the correction in another life of the injustices in this one.

Meaning

Without God, human life is without meaning. To understand the meaning of something is to fit it into a context, to relate it to other reality within that context, especially to its analog. But what is man's context? If God is removed from the picture and we have no transcendent frame of reference, we can understand ourselves only in terms of what is less than human. Konrad Lorenz did a study of the pecking order among geese, and others trot this study out as an explanation of human behavior.[7] Aggression, sex, territoriality are all advanced by some of our contemporaries as the model for understanding man.[8] In each case we are invited to gaze into a reductive mirror and recognize the jungle as our lost kingdom. What is left out of all these theories of man is the qualities that distinguish us from the lower creation and that we admire and respect as being most humane: our striving for truth, justice, love, and beauty. Without God, to whom these qualities relate us (who indeed implanted them within us), these qualities have no objective correlative in the universe; they are an inexplicable quirk of evolution related to nothing else in reality whatsoever.

A second aspect of meaning is purpose. Man is the meaning-giver to the lower creation, but what gives meaning to man? Man names the other creatures, but who names man? Is there a need for man in the universe? Each of us contrives purposes of his own, but is there for any of us a purpose we cannot contrive but only discover? Is mankind a purposeful contrivance or only a cosmic accident? Is there a cosmic creator and lover who has hopes and dreams for us or are we merely an aberrant race of intelligent ants clinging to a blue-green rock in the midst of a vast, dark, lifeless void? Life is a struggle, for what purpose? It is painful to be born, frustrating to learn to walk and talk. It is difficult for a child to learn the rules of civilized behavior let alone those of math and English grammar. The dating and mating game is fraught with embarrassment, rejection, and humiliation as well as happier events. Child-rearing and pursuit of a career are both difficult and anxious. Even after one's children are happily grown and mated, if they are, one then begins fretting about one's grandchildren over whose lives one has no control at all. And if, after long years of service and sweat, you become a great success in your career, you then must retire. And then you die. And what has been the point of it all? If we do not live our hour upon the stage against a cosmic backdrop, then Macbeth had the right review of our act:

> Tomorrow, and tomorrow and tomorrow
> Creeps in this petty pace from day to day
> To the last syllable of recorded time;
> And all our yesterdays have lighted fools
> The way to dusty death. Out, out, brief candle!

Life's but a walking shadow, a poor player
That struts and frets his hour upon the stage
And then is heard no more: it is a tale
Told by an idiot, full of sound and fury,
Signifying nothing.[9]

A PRELIMINARY DEFINITION

None of the above proves God—but does give us an idea of what is at stake and thus what a meaningful definition of the word *God* would be. Whatever else God is, he is at least Ultimate Being who was before all worlds, who causes to be all that is, and who will be when nothing else, save those who live in him, any longer is. He is the origin and aim of human being. He is the Creator of human nature with its limitations and possibilities, the Word who calls us into being and calls us to himself, the Power who energizes human life and impregnates it with his own life. There is, then, a divine definition of humanity and a purpose for us in relation to which our lives may be judged good or bad or both. There is at least the possibility that justice will ultimately be done and the fruits of love not lost.

The Trinity

To know the meaning of the word *God* is not to know God. And even to understand the necessity of God in order to make sense of life is not to prove God. As we have seen, God can be known but he cannot be proven. The universe did not arrive at God; it started from him and perhaps we must do the same. What the Christian Church offers, on the basis of her almost four thousand years' acquaintance with him, is not a proof but an invitation to a life of faith in him and with him. But who is he?

The first thing the Church might say about God is "We do not know who he is in himself. How could we?" Does my cat know who I am? He knows me in relationship to himself: he knows that I am the source of his food; he knows that I can let him in and out of doors. He may by observation and analogy know that I am sleeping when he sees me sleeping or eating when he sees me eating. He surely has no idea of what I am doing when he sees me reading and of course would have no idea at all of what I am thinking when I put the book down. God transcends us much more than we transcend the cats. It is much easier to say what God is not than to say what he is. The cats at least can observe us; we cannot observe God but only his glory. Cats can sit in our laps and rub themselves up against our legs; we cannot touch God. The cats, like us, live and die but God does not pass in and out of being. Whatever we learn of God, we know that we shall never be able to wrap our minds around him. In other words God is invisible, intangible, immortal, and incomprehensible. To put all this more positively, God is mystery in the strict sense of the word; he is not only unknown but also intrinsically unknowable (*saber*). He remains mysterious even in revelation; to know him (*conocer*) is to be acquainted with mystery.

What we can know is not who God is in himself but who God is in relationship to us. We can speak of him as he has revealed himself to us. This the Church does in the doctrine of the Trinity. But even St. Augustine, who wrote a book on the Trinity, cautions us that the Church speaks of the Trinity not so much to say something as to avoid saying nothing.[10]

GOD THE FATHER

To speak of the Trinity is to speak of three movements of the one divine Being, three ways in which God goes about being God. God the Father is the abyss of the Godhead, infinitely mysterious yet called "Father" because from him the other persons of the Godhead proceed and from him all creation receives its being. "The Father, as primordial Being, is the depth of the mystery of God. We could not possibly know anything of him 'in himself', we know him only in so far as he does pour himself out in the dynamics of Being and is revealed in and through the other persons [of the Trinity] who are joined with him in the unity of Being."[11] By way of analogy, consider the sun. All life on earth depends upon it. As my gardener recently explained to me, "the sun is what makes plants do their thing." Were the sun to blink out, a preternatural darkness would immediately descend upon our planet and the temperature would begin plummeting toward absolute zero. Long before the earth's temperature reaches that point, where all molecular activity stops, life on earth would be extinct, within a matter of hours. But how does the sun, being 93,000,000 miles away from us, do this? The sun's energy is brought to bear upon this planet, creating and sustaining earthly life, by the sun's light and heat. Just so is God the Father brought to us, and we to him, by God the Son through God the Holy Spirit. And just as sunlight and heat are not other than the sun itself radiating from itself, God the Son and Holy Spirit are not other than God. They are God himself emanating from himself. And just as there was never a time when the sun existed but sunlight and heat did not, so God the Son and God the Holy Spirit are co-eternal with God the Father.[12]

GOD THE SON

God the Son, the Logos, the Word, is the structuring agent of creation. The Word expresses the mind of the Godhead and is the source both of the rational order of creation and of human reason. He is the reason that creation is knowable and that we have the capacity for knowledge. He is the legislator both of the natural physical law discovered by scientists and of the natural moral law discerned by philosophers and revealed to Moses on Sinai. He is the Word who spoke through the prophets and became incarnate in Jesus of Nazareth. Though he was the agent of revelation in the Old Testament, he himself is revealed overtly in the New Testament.

GOD THE HOLY SPIRIT

God the Holy Spirit, like God the Son, is a dynamic of the Godhead and is God in relation to us. But the Logos is the source of reason, while the Spirit is the inspirer of non-rational creativity. The Logos makes the scientist's work possible; the

Spirit inspires the poet. If the Word is the law giver, the Spirit is the life giver. The Spirit is free, elusive like the wind. The Logos is the source of the routine and dependable; the Spirit surprises us. He is unpredictable and unsettling. The Holy Spirit is also known, simply, as Love. It is to the Holy Spirit we sing the hymn "Come down, O Love divine, seek thou this soul of mine, and visit it with thine own ardor glowing; O Comforter, draw near, within my heart appear, and kindle it, thy holy flame bestowing. O let it freely burn, till earthly passions turn to dust and ashes in its heat consuming."[13] St. Augustine spoke of the Holy Spirit as the love shared between the Father and the Son.[14] Love is the power that unites two persons without destroying the identity of either. We must speak of the Holy Spirit again when speaking of our salvation; for love is also the power that overcomes estrangement between two persons who belong together but are separated. The theologian John Macquarrie speaks of the Father as primordial Being, the Son as expressive Being, and the Spirit as unitive Being.[15]

The Holy Spirit has also been associated with Wisdom. If the Logos is the revealer from without, the Spirit is the revealer from within. If the Logos is the source of reason, the Spirit is the source of intuition.

ONE GOD

It would of course be a great mistake to set the work of one person of the Trinity off against that of the other persons. This is true for two reasons. First, the work of the persons is complementary. Where would we be without either the right or left sides of our brain? Where would we be without either reason or intuition? Law is for the sake of freedom, and no freedom may be finally had without law. Structure is for the sake of dynamics: without my skeleton, I would be a blob; but with only my skeleton, I would be dead. Second, the whole Godhead is involved in the work of each person. For example, God the Father is particularly associated with creation—so much so that he is often called "the Creator." The Nicene Creed begins, "We believe in one God, the Father, the Almighty, maker of heaven and earth, of all that is, seen and unseen."[16] However, in the Genesis account of creation, God creates through the Word, and the Spirit is hovering over the process. The Trinity works as a team. If we want to credit our creation to the Father, he will point to the Son and Holy Spirit. If we credit our redemption to the Son, he will point to the Father and Spirit. If we credit our sanctification to the Holy Spirit, he will point to the Father and Son. In each case the recipient of our gratitude will point to the other persons of the Trinity and say, "I couldn't have done it without them."

People sometimes find the Trinity to be puzzling mathematically. What does it mean to speak of three persons in one substance? Perhaps a helpful analogy would be the space of the room you are sitting in. The space has three dimensions, height, length and width. Each dimension comprises all the space in the room. For example, all the space in the room is part of the room's height; you cannot pick any point in the room through which you cannot draw a line from floor to ceiling. But likewise, every point in the space is part of the room's width; you can draw a line from wall to wall through any point in the room. The same is true of the room's length. Just so, all of God is the Father; all of God is the Son and all of God is the Holy Spirit.

Though all the space in the room is comprised by each dimension, all three dimensions are necessary to the space being what it is. Without any one of the dimensions, you would be a smear on a flat plane. Just so each person in the Trinity is necessary to God being who he is. If God were only the Father, he would be infinitely remote. If he were only the Son, Jesus would be idolized. If God were only the Spirit, he would be amorphous. But without the Father, God would not be ultimate; without the Son, he would be unintelligible; without the Spirit, we could have no intimacy with him. The God whom the Christian Church invites us into faithful relationship with is one God in three persons. Each of the persons is fully God; each person is necessary to the fullness of God.

To restate the whole matter in terms of everyday experience, I have found that the word *God* means different things to different people. To some people God is the infinite mysterious creative reality that lies behind and beyond all other reality. They point to babies, flowers, and microbes; they point to the innumerable galaxies spread over millions of light-years of space; and they say, "It had to come from somewhere." To others, God is a person. He is that person who called Abraham to be a pilgrim upon earth. He is that person who called a people into being in revealing his holy will to them through Moses and in entering into a covenant with them at Sinai. He is pre-eminently that person made known to us in the life of Jesus of Nazareth; thus, he is a person wholly righteous and wholly compassionate. He is that person who conquers death and overcomes sin. To still others, the word God denotes a power, a dynamic—not an external force remote in time and space, but an intimate, felt force within us, closer to us than we are to ourselves. God is a force of love that draws two people into intimacy and unites a community. He is a force of vitality that makes us swell within and know intuitively that the life we are experiencing in that moment is eternal. He is a force of wisdom inspiring the poet, giving the flash of insight to the scientist and gently leading to discernment the community that puts itself at the disposal of God's will. The doctrine of the Trinity tells us that these three "Gods" are one. It is the same Ultimate Reality that we experience as (1) the infinite, mysterious, creative Reality lying behind and beyond all other reality, (2) the Person who initiates a personal relationship with us and, (3) the felt force of life, love and wisdom. God the Father is God beyond us; God the Son is God beside us; God the Holy Spirit is God within us. They are the Holy Trinity, One God.

The Personality of God

Language was forged in our interaction with things of this world, especially things that can be seen and touched. Speaking of God who is infinite, invisible and intangible burdens our language and stretches human imagination. The Bible has an ambivalent attitude toward images of God. On one hand, the second commandment (Ex. 20:4) absolutely prohibits any graven image, that is any painted or sculpted image, of God. Thus the ancient Hebrews were never known for their art and sculpture, and Jewish temples and synagogues to this day are largely devoid of it. On the other, the Bible contains an incomparably rich treasury of verbal images of God. *King, judge, warrior, savior, father, lover* are all words coined originally to refer to human beings and used symbolically in the Bible to refer to God. Almost all religious language is intrinsically symbolic because it is imagining the unimaginable and making vivid the invisible.

The Bible does not see God as a featureless force, a vast sea, as some eastern religions do. The Biblical God is emphatically personal. Is God's personhood to be taken literally? Yes and no. On one hand, we do not want to say that God is a person; for that would make him finite—one being no matter how great among other beings. On the other, God can hardly be less than personal. "He that planted the ear, does he not hear? He that formed the eye, does he not see?" (Ps. 94:9) Science describes the process of higher life being built out of lower, organic molecules from inorganic just as we might watch a beautiful cathedral being built out of unimposing blocks of stone. But just as the cathedral requires the mind of an architect who is a higher form of being than either the stones or the cathedral, so does the creation. Furthermore, our fathers in the faith have spoken of God as personal because they experienced him as such. So we attribute personal qualities, such as consciousness and will, to God by analogy. It is more adequate to call God personal than to call him impersonal. Some theologians call him transpersonal. But transpersonal is so technical a term I find it more helpful to think of God as a vast ocean with personality.

A still greater problem resides in the traditional use, which I have continued, of the masculine pronoun *he* in referring to God. The Church has never thought or taught that God is male. Even the ancient Hebrews were aware that God created both sexes in his image (Gen. 1:26–27). God is beyond the sexual division that characterizes humankind. Conversely, qualities we think of as masculine and feminine both have their analogue in the Godhead. It is equally misleading to refer to God as *he* or *she*, though either would be preferable to *it*.

What sort of person is God? Reason led St. Thomas Aquinas to the insight that God's essence was to be (*esse*); revelation gave him the insight that God's essence is to love (*amare*).[17] St. John wrote, "Dear friends, let us love one another, because love is from God . . . . For God is love." (I St. Jn. 4:7,9); and St. Isaac the Syrian wrote: "Love is the kingdom which the Lord mystically promised to the disciples, when he said that they would eat in his kingdom: 'You shall eat and drink in my kingdom' (Lk. 22:30). What should they eat and drink if not love?"

"When we have reached love, we have reached God and our journey is complete. We have crossed over to the island which lies beyond the world, where are the Father, the Son and the Holy Spirit: to whom be glory and dominion."[18]

Because love is the nature of ultimate reality, truth is finally relational not propositonal. God's attributes are properly seen as functions of his personality; they are all divine love in action. Some of his attributes are as follows.

GRACIOUS

God's graciousness and all the aspects of his love will be major themes of the rest of this book, but for the moment let us merely note that the creation is an act of grace. The creation is a freely willed act of God; no one makes him do it. Paradoxically, it might equally well be argued that the creation is an inevitable fruit of the ecstatic love the persons of the Trinity have among themselves; the creation is an effulgence of divine love. But in God there is no distinction between essence and act; he is what he does. For us too, did we but see it, freedom is not the ability to act contrary to our nature; freedom is not perversion. Freedom is the ability to be who we are, to act according to our nature, to actually be ourselves. Creation is grace in a second sense as well. "Existence is always a gift from God—a free gift of his love, a gift that is never taken back, but a gift none the less, not something that we possess by our own power. God alone has the cause and source of his being in himself; all created things have their cause and source, not in themselves but in him."[19]

PROVIDENTIAL

To say that God is providential is not to say that he controls everything that happens. He has choreographed the evolutionary dance so as to allow room for improvisation. Chance, which is the sub-human version of freedom, has its role in creation. To say that God is providential is to say that he is hospitable,

bountiful, extraordinarily generous; he has stocked the larder
with provisions. The earth supports an incredible variety of life
teeming in every nook and cranny. When man, with the aid of
his modern technology, goes to Antarctica, he finds he has been
preceded there by penguins. When we had developed pressure
hulls strong enough to withstand the enormous forces of the
Marianas Trench, we descended to the depths of the Pacific
Ocean only to find already there some weird luminescent fish
living their fishy lives. Big animals mark off huge swatches of
land as "their territory," but the spaces between the big animals
are in fact filled with little animals and the space between them
filled with insects and the space between them filled with
microbes. God's providence is an expression of the exuberant
generosity of his love. It is as if he had said, "Let there be life!
Let no space go uninhabited and let nothing be lost." Life is
never wasted; the life of every plant and every animal, upon its
death, goes to fertilize the soil or feed another animal. Perhaps
the Psalmist hymned God's providence best:

You have set the earth upon its foundations so that it never
shall move at any time . . . .

You send springs into the valleys;
they flow between the mountains.
All the beasts of the field drink their fill from them,
and the wild asses quench their thirst.
Beside them the birds of the air make their nests
and sing among the branches.
You water the mountains from your dwelling on high;
the earth is fully satisfied by the fruit of your works.

You make grass grow for flocks and herds

and plants to serve mankind;

That they may bring food from the earth,

and wine to gladden our hearts,

Oil to make a cheerful countenance,

and bread to strengthen the heart.

The trees of the Lord are full of sap,

the cedars of Lebanon which he plants,

In which the birds build their nests,

and in whose tops the stork makes his dwelling.

The high hills are a refuge for the mountain goats,

and the stony cliffs for the rock badgers.

You make darkness that it may be night,

in which all the beasts of the forest prowl.

The lion roar after their prey

and seek their food from God . . . .

All of them look to you

to give them their food in due season.

You give it to them; they gather it;

you open your hand, and they are filled with good things.

You hide your face, and they are terrified;

you take away their breath, and they die and return to their dust.

You send forth your Spirit, and they are created;

and so you renew the face of the earth (Ps. 104:5, 10–22, 28–31).

POWERFUL

Here above all we must be wary of imposing human ideas upon God. We tend to think of qualities we admire and attribute them to God in the nth degree as a matter of definition. Hence God's "omnipotence." We think as a matter of course that God must be all powerful else he cannot be God. But this thinking is surely both arrogant and false. If God is, he is. He is who he is regardless of whether he matches our preconceptions of divinity. In practice God's power is limited both by the finitude of the creation and by human freedom. These limitations will be discussed in Chapters III and IV.

We might first consider what we mean by the word power. We all too often mean the ability to bend reality to our will, to impose our will upon recalcitrant circumstances or people. Our image of power is the conqueror who can destroy his enemies or, better yet, has done so. We spend billions of dollars each year acquiring more power to devastate other nations. During the Cold War, the United States and the Soviet Union stood facing each other like two men hip deep in gasoline. One held ten matches in his hand and the other twelve. Each was sure that what he most needed were more matches. This is power? Is the ability to coerce and destroy really so powerful after all? Any fool with an axe can kill a tree. But who can create one? When my house was built, some grass on the lot was an inconvenient obstacle to the builder's desire to lay down a driveway; so he killed it with whatever version of Agent Orange they used back then and they laid down an asphalt driveway.

The years went by and the sun shone and the rains fell and the asphalt cracked and up through the cracks, grass poked out its head saying "Remember me? I'm back." The problem I have with my house is that I have to keep painting it, repairing it, shoring up its foundation, in other words, work constantly to keep it from falling down. I have the opposite problem with the yard. It keeps growing. I have to work constantly to chop it back to a non-threatening size, to keep it from getting out of control. Why the difference? It is simply that man made the house and God made the grass and God is a lot more powerful than we are.

Suppose that the only power God has is the power of love and the kinds of power that flow from love, like the power to create. Love holds the creation in being in every moment as we shall see in the next chapter. Suppose God has no power to punish or destroy except by withdrawing his love, which he cannot do without ceasing to be himself. A friend of mine went to confession trembling with terror because of his many sins. "What are you so afraid of?" his confessor asked; "There is nothing out there but love." Ever since, my friend has gone to confession regularly to bathe in the continuing stream of grace.

Theoklitos of Dionysiou described the nature of ultimate reality thus:

> There is one truth that reigns supreme from the fringes of the throne of glory down to the least shadow of the most insignificant of creatures: that one truth is Love. Love is the source from which the holy streams of grace flow down unceasingly from the City of God,

watering the earth and making it fruitful. "One deep calls to another" (Ps. 42:7): like a deep, or an abyss, in its infinity love helps us picture to ourselves the dread vision of the Godhead. It is love that fashions all things and holds them in unity. It is love that gives life and warmth, that inspires and guides. Love is the seal set upon creation, the signature of the Creator. Love is the explanation of his handiwork.[20]

III. Creation

"In the beginning of creation, when God made heaven and earth, the earth was without form and void, with darkness over the face of the abyss, and the spirit of God hovering over the surface of the waters" (Gen. 1:1f). So begins the Biblical account of creation. Off and on in this century we have been treated to an asinine debate between "creationism" and the theory of evolution. The debate is asinine first because it pits against each other two things that

III. CREATION
A. Substance
   1) MATTER
      (a) Energy of the Spirit
      (b) Force of Love
         i. The Strong Force
         ii. The Electromagnetic Force
         iii. Gravity
   2) FORM
B. Finitude
   1) LIMITS
      (a) Natural Law
      (b) Matter Is Breakable
      (c) Things Take Time
   2) GOODNESS
   3) MORALITY
C. The Creation as Grace
   1) GRACE
      (a) Meaning
      (b) Response
      (c) Original Grace
   2) STEWARDSHIP
      (a) Gratitude
      (b) Property
      (c) Economic Ethics
   3) SACRAMENT
      (a) Meaning
      (b) Creation
      (c) Idolatry
D. A Song of Creation

are not incompatible. The theory of evolution does not deny God's creation of the universe; rather, it attempts to describe the process of that creation. The debate is asinine secondly because it confuses the provinces of science and theology.

Science is in the business of building useful intellectual models of natural phenomena—models that economically describe our experience of phenomena and can accurately predict future experience. Science is a particularly useful approach to those aspects of reality that are repetitive and quantifiable. It is not a helpful approach to those aspects of reality that defy quantification, the phenomenon of love, for example, which is obviously as real as the paper this book is printed on. Were a scientist to say that anything that does not yield itself to the scientific method is unreal, he would not be making a scientific statement but a philosophical one. It would be equally unscientific to say that evolution has proceeded without direction or that there is no purpose in the universe other than that we humans bring to it.

"Christian theology seeks to think the Church's faith as a coherent whole. It aims not only at showing the internal coherence of the Christian faith, that is to say, how the several doctrines constitute a unity, but also at exhibiting the coherence of this faith with the many other beliefs and attitudes to which we are committed in the modern world. Only if these tasks are accomplished can the faith be held intelligently and be integrated with the whole range of human life."[1] The theologian has no business trying to construct a scientific model of the physical world. Rather than do bad science and call it theology, the theologian is to reflect upon the contemporary scientific model in the light of his faith; that is, he views the model under the aspect of eternity and in the context of our relationship with God. That is precisely what the author of Genesis was doing in his day and it is what I shall be doing in this chapter.

Substance

MATTER

As we look out upon the world we must be impressed by the seemingly infinite variety of realities that make up reality, realities as disparate as sunflowers and the sun, as different as snowflakes and human beings. But the variety does not end there. Each snowflake is unique, different from every other of the millions upon millions of snowflakes that fall each day. Also no two of the more than six billion people in the world look exactly alike. One of the major thrusts of science since its beginnings in ancient Greece has been the search for substance, for common denominators which underlie the variety of realities we see. What does modern science say about the stuff from which reality is made and about the glue that binds the stuff together into the world we know?

Energy of the spirit

Science has discovered that all of the trillions of distinct realities in the universe are made up of less than seven million compounds, the ultimate unit of which is the molecule. More amazingly, science has discovered that all of the seven million different types of molecules are themselves made up of different combination of only about one hundred elements, the ultimate unit of each of which is the atom.[2]

By the time I was in school, in the 1950's, science had made a still more startling discovery: the hundred atoms themselves are made up of different combinations of perhaps only three particles—protons, neutrons and electrons. Having discovered these building blocks of matter, what did science say about them? The particles are described in terms of three distinguishing characteristics: mass, charge and spin. The rest mass of an electron is assigned the number 1. The rest mass of a proton is 1836. That of a neutron is 1837. Though the proton is 1836 times as massive as an electron, that does not mean it is bigger. A pound of lead has the same mass but less volume than a pound of feathers does. Mass is measured in electron volts, which are a measure of energy. In other words, mass is just a form of energy. Whatever happened to our solid world? Mass is energy condensed into lumps as it were. Einstein worked out the formula for the equivalence: $E=mc^2$.

The second characteristic of particles is charge. The proton has a positive electrical charge; the electron has a negative one. The neutron has no charge, hence its name. Charge determines how a particle will react in the presence of other particles; like lovers, opposites attract. Electric charge comes in only one fixed amount. Each of these three particles has either one whole unit of charge, two whole units or none at all. No particle can have one and a half units. Why this is so is one of the many unanswered questions in present-day physics. The fact that reality comes in discreet units led one wag to say that God made the positive integers and man made all the other numbers like fractions.

The third characteristic of particles is their spin. They always spin at exactly the same rate. "The rate of spin is such a fundamental characteristic of subatomic particles that if it is altered, the particle itself is destroyed."[3] This fact has made some physicists wonder if the different particles might just be different states of motion of some underlying substance. Like charge, and energy in general, spin is quantized; it comes in discrete units. Spin is measured by angular momentum, which is the effort it would take to stop the spin. Finally, spin is a metaphor. Max Born wrote, "The angular momentum of a subatomic particle is fixed, definite and known. But one should not imagine that there is anything in the nature of matter actually rotating."[4]

To summarize, the entire universe is composed of protons, neutrons and electrons that are characterized by mass, charge and spin. What is mass? Condensed energy. What is charge? Electrical energy. What is spin? Energy. What finally lies at the heart of that matter the universe is made of? Energy. *Energy* is the word in the scientist's vocabulary that comes closest to the meaning of the religious word *spirit*. There are some naive folk in our culture who account themselves too sophisticated to believe in the reality of something so mysterious, invisible and intangible as spirit. The materialist points the finger to what can be seen and touched and says, "There and there alone is reality." But the finger he points and the rock he points to are alike composed of invisible atoms, which are mainly empty space but which have at their centers bundles of positively charged energy and have in orbit around these nuclei clouds of negatively charged energy. What has been going on over the last 15 billion years is the incarnation of energy into matter and the slow orchestration of increasingly complex forms of matter. Creation is the process of spirit becoming flesh until finally in man the spirit is incarnate in flesh that is aware of also being spirit.

Of whose energy is matter made? Whose but God's? Whose but his could it be? How much energy did God put into creation of the earth? Take the sum total of mass in and on the earth, multiply it by 186,326 squared and you have the beginning of your answer. He has put a lot of energy into making us. Why did he do it?

Force of love

Why does not the universe consist of just a cloud of energy or of just trillions of subatomic particles floating randomly about? The glue that binds the protons, electrons and neutrons into atoms, that binds the atoms into molecules and that binds heavenly bodies into solar systems and galaxies are three forces: the strong force, the electromagnetic force, and the force of gravity. I mention them in order of strength.

The strong force is the strongest of the three and operates within the nuclei of atoms. The nucleus of most atoms consists of a clump of neutrons, which have no electrical charge and a clump of protons, which have a positive charge. Positive charges repel each other as we see when we try to put the positive poles of two magnets together. The protons should repel each other and fly off in different directions. But they do not because the strong force overcomes the tendency to fly away. No one knows why the force is there. Nor do we really know how it works. The strong force is the shortest range of all the forces; it will capture a proton aimed at the nucleus only once the proton gets to within one ten-trillionth of a centimeter (10^{-13}cm) of the nucleus.

The next strongest force is the electromagnetic one familiar to us all from the phenomenon of magnetism. It is what keeps the magnet on the refrigerator door (though mine usually fall off). More importantly, it is what glues atoms of different elements together to form the seven million different molecules which in turn make up snowflakes and humans. For example, an atom of sodium and an atom of chlorine join to form a molecule of salt by sharing an electron. This is the force that would make protons repel each other were not the strong force one hundred times stronger.

The weakest of the forces (10^{42} weaker than the electromagnetic force), and the one that operates at the longest range, is gravity. It is the subtlest of the forces because it affects the shape of time and space, the arena of reality. We know that gravity is a force of attraction between masses. If you stepped out of a flying airplane, you and the earth would rush to meet each other. Since you are much less massive than the earth, you would do most of the traveling. We know that the strength of gravity is directly proportional to the masses involved and inversely proportional to the square of the distance between them. In other words, the farther you are from the earth, the less attraction you have for each other; if you get far enough away, you need not come back.

"The grand unification theory holds that all . . . of nature's basic forces have evolved from a single force which was created in the first flashes of the 'big bang', the cosmic explosion that created the universe."[5] I suspect that the force preceded the creation, that it has been from before all time, that it is eternal, that it is the force of love, the Holy Spirit himself binding the Father and Son together in eternal union. Creative love is the force that binds the protons and the electrons together, preserving the being and identity of each, yet creating a new and greater reality-an atom of sodium perhaps, an atom of chlorine perhaps. It is divine love that binds together atoms of volatile sodium and poisonous chlorine to create the healthful salt and does so without annihilating either the sodium or the chlorine. It is the Holy Spirit that preserves the identity and integrity of a man and a woman and yet makes them one flesh creating a new and greater reality, the human family. It is the Holy Spirit that preserves Christian families yet binds them together into Christ's Body, the Church. It is Love that preserves the sun and planets in being yet binds them together into the solar system making life possible on earth, giving light and heat for growth and knowledge. In sum, God's love binds spirit into complex matter and sustains us in being in every moment. Were God to withdraw his love from us, even for an instant, the universe would literally fall apart, our particles collapsing into primordial chaos.

The three persons of the holy Trinity have a common substance, God. Might the three fundamental particles and the three fundamental forces have a common substance as well? Physicists have been seeking it. Some of them report that "the fundamental entity turns out not to be a particle like the electron, infinitely small and of zero dimensionality, but a string, like a rubber band, infinitely thin but with a tiny bit of length. The typical length of one of these hypothesized strings is 10^{-33} centimeters, one hundredth of a billionth of a billionth of the size of the nucleus of an atom. A primal string is smaller than an atomic nucleus by the same factor that an atomic nucleus is smaller than Rhode Island. According to theory, all these ultra-small strings are identical. But each of them can vibrate in different ways, similar to the vibrations of a guitar string, and the different notes thus produced create all the different forces and particles in nature. One pattern of vibration corresponds to the gravitational force; another corresponds to the electron, and so on."[6] So, the creation may be music that God is orchestrating from a string section unimaginably small.

FORM

The Holy Spirit does not throw atoms and molecules and people together just any old which way. All creatures have a specific form. Men and women have two arms and two legs and, when they reproduce, their children do. The human form is passed along to the next generation in accordance with the laws of genetics. Without order, form, proportion, we would have not creation but chaos. Shakespeare's deformed King Richard III described himself thus: "I that am curtail'd of this fair proportion, cheated of feature by dissembling nature, deform'd, unfinish'd, sent before my time into this breathing world scarce half made up . . . . Why, love forswore me in my mother's womb and did corrupt frail nature . . . to shape my legs of an unequal size . . . to disproportion me in every part, like to a chaos!"[7]

Water was symbolic of chaos to the ancient Hebrews because it had no apparent form. One could not grab hold of it. It was itself shapeless, assuming the shape of whatever contained it. But could it be contained? The Psalmist praised the Creator in these words:

You covered [the earth] with the Deep as with a mantle;

the waters stood higher than the mountains.

At your rebuke they fled;

at the voice of your thunder they hastened away.

They went up into the hills and down to the valleys beneath,

to the places you had appointed for them.

You set the limits they should not pass;

they shall not again cover the earth. (Ps. 104:6–9)

A flood threatened to undo creation, returning it to chaos. Conversely, creation consisted of forming order out of chaos: "In the beginning of creation, when God made heaven and earth, the earth was without form and void . . ." (Gen. 1:1–2).

The informing dynamic of the Godhead is the Logos, the Word, God the Son, the Second Person of the Trinity. He is the architect of creation who draws the blueprints for the mechanics of nature and makes the genetic code. He directs the Holy Spirit, if you will, which bits of matter to bind to which other bits. His directions are imprinted in nature itself; his laws are implicit in the creation. By carefully studying nature, science abstracts natural laws from it, thus reading the mind of

God. One of the great mind readers was Galileo who in 1629 published his *Dialogues concerning the Two Principle Systems of the World, the Ptolemaic and the Copernican* in which he persuasively argued that the earth revolved around the sun not vice versa. But the Bible said otherwise; so the Church forced Galileo to "abjure, curse and detest" his "errors and heresies." I am sure the Church thought she was doing God a favor; I am equally sure God was not pleased. After all, it was he who made the earth go around the sun in the first place. If he had wanted the sun to go around the earth, he would have done the creation differently.

All anti-intellectualism is anti-God because his is the original intellect. All genuine knowledge is knowledge of divine activity or its consequences. Cosmology, biology, ontology, all ology is ology of the Logos.

A final note of caution: It must not be thought that because the energy of which matter is made comes from God or because the Logos informs and the Spirit unifies creation, God himself is the ultimate substance of creation. All my children's genes come from their mother and me but that does not mean that they are we. They have reality of their own. By providing food, shelter and clothing I sustain them in my human way and even have the ability to destroy them but they are their own people, having an existence quite independent of me; they think their own thoughts. So too an artist's creation, once done, has an identity and reality independent of the artist. Though the energy that is the substance of the creation is from God, it is not itself God. Though the creation is dependent upon God's substance in every instant, it has its own reality and identity apart from him.

Finitude

LIMITS

One obvious difference between God and the creation is that he is infinite and the creation is finite. We think of God as unlimited in power but the creation has very specific limits that impose limits upon God's ability to work within it. Any creation would. He could have made a different universe than the one he did but any one he made would have its own set of limits.

Natural Law

Form imposes limits. Matter once formed is not infinitely malleable. No one can make a silk purse out of a sow's ear. Natural law is prohibitory as well as permissive. The same chemical structure that enables sodium to combine with chlorine prevents it from combining with argon. The specific genetic structure that enables horses to pass along their horsiness to foals prevents them from reproducing with cattle. The elbow that enables me to bend my forearm to my chest prevents me from bending it in the opposite direction. Natural laws could not be suddenly suspended or over-ridden without plunging the creation into chaos. If the engine on the airplane I am riding suddenly conks out, I do not look for God to suspend the law of gravity for my sake; his breaking that law would cause many more deaths than mine.

Matter Is Breakable

It is amazing the world works as well as it does. My body, which is God-made, works much more reliably than my car, which is man-made and much less complicated. But my body is breakable. The more complicated something is the more things can go wrong with it. Our bodies are complicated indeed, far more complicated than anything we can make. A virus in a pregnant woman or exposure to too much radiation can knock genes askew and produce deformity in her child. Moreover my body, like my car, has built-in obsolescence. It is clearly not intended to last much longer than four score years, if that. Any fool can cut down a tree. And we have finally figured out how to smash even atoms. Man, the acme of God's creation, has become very clever about destroying it. Matter is breakable.

Things Take Time

God does not accomplish his purposes instantaneously. When he wanted to free his people from bondage in Egypt, he did not just snap his fingers and magically transport them to the promised land. He had to work at it, and it took time. When he set out to create a universe, he needed a little patience. Science says the universe began about 15 billion years ago but the earth has been functioning for only the last 5. The intervening 10 billion years were needed to forge the elements within several generations of stars. Life on earth has been evolving for only the last 3.5 billion years, and creatures we would recognize as fellow humans have graced our planet for less than 4 million years. "Why so long?" I once asked a sage.[8] "Are you in a hurry?" he replied. God is clearly not. And besides, things take time. And the worlds evolve partly by chance, which, like human freedom, was perhaps necessary for God to grant in order that the world, like us, should have its own identity, its measure of independence from him.

GOODNESS

The creation is not perfect. In the long evolution of life on this planet there have been many dead ends, much trial and error so to speak. In this sense we must say that not everything God has done has turned out well. And things now do not always work as intended; deformed babies are born every day. Is deformity part of God's plan? Only in the sense that the creation is his plan and the creation is necessarily finite and thus carries within it the potential for deformity. So, God is ultimately responsible for deformed children. But it is nonsense to suggest that God intends deformity any more than I intend whatever errors are in this book. The form that God intends is obvious from the form most babies have. God does not willingly subvert his own creation.

The creation is also not perfected in the sense that it is not yet what it shall be. The earth is alive geologically. At its core the earth is molten not inert. Our continents and seas ride upon plates that shift about and crash into each other producing earthquakes and volcanic eruptions. It makes little sense for us to build our cities upon geological fault lines and in the shadow of volcanoes and then complain when the earth acts as is intended. And would we wish the earth to be no longer evolving? Would it be a good thing, that is, a desirable thing for the earth to be perfected, to be inert, geologically dead? Evolution of life has progressed by mutation—technically, deformity—of what preceded it. In other words, perfection is not always good.

Is creation good? God must think so else he would not love us so, keeping us in being from moment to moment. He could be rid of us in a flash if he so desired. The Bible confirms our Creator's delight at the work of his hands. At each stage it pleased him. On the sixth day, "God saw all that he had made, and it was very good" (Gen. 1:31, cf. 1:4,10,12,18, 21, 25).

But do we agree? People sometimes say, "If God made this world, he sure did a crummy job of it." I want to know: Could you do better? Which animal can you improve upon? Make us a better lion or even a better mouse. If that is too difficult, fashion a tree or even a leaf.[9] Do you in fact do a better job of the things you are in charge of? And if you say, "I could do a better job if I were God," I wonder how you can possibly know that. An artist is judged by what he does with the materials he works with. A sculptor can do some things with marble and other things with metal. Each material has its own possibilities and limitations. What material would you forge to make a world if you were God? What different matter would you invent and what limitations would it have? Which law of nature would you repeal or which force revoke? Gravity? Why, we would all fly off the earth. One would think that those most critical of the creation would be most energetic in improving upon it, developing new breeds of cattle and strains of plants. One would expect to see them in the vanguard of charitable enterprises, rushing to alleviate the suffering caused by earthquake, fire and flood. But my experience has been the opposite. The critics stay home and nurse their bitterness. It is those who love nature who improve upon it; those who embrace life who add to it.

The goodness of the creation is not finally an intellectual question but an existential decision. No one has to live in this world. We each have the option of suicide. The most basic faith decision anyone ever makes is either to affirm the world with all its terror and grandeur or to flee from it into self-deception, alcoholism or suicide. The question "Is the creation good?" is equivalent to the question "Is life in it desirable?" We answer with our lives.

MORALITY

We are still focusing upon the sub-human creation, but it is not too early to ask if there is a morality evident in it. Since Darwin first showed us that in dealing with nature we are dealing with history, much effort has been focused upon drawing lessons from evolution. Nature was said to be red in tooth and claw. The law of the jungle was held to be the law of life. Survival of the fittest was nature's norm, and social Darwinists held it stupid to protect the weak or subsidize the incompetent. In recent decades more facts have been assembled and soberer conclusions drawn. Nature is not nearly so pugnacious as we once imagined. Vast groups of animals of various kinds co-inhabit the same land peacefully. Intra-specific warfare is rarely fatal and inter-specific relations usually pacific. Most animals are not predacious, and those who are kill only to eat (man excepted). We have seen how much energy goes into making a bit of matter and how long it took for life to evolve. Among the earlier and lower forms of creatures, it takes much life to make a little. A fish will lay hundreds of eggs to have a few survive to maturity; a turtle will need to lay only a bit fewer. But as we progress up the evolutionary ladder, we see an increasing inclination and ability of creatures to protect their young. Birds brood upon their eggs and will distract or attack dangers to them. Mammals keep their young within their own bodies until the progeny are ready to "hatch." The direction and moral of evolution is from survival of the fittest to protection of the weak. To man, who has the wit to hear it, the will of God is made explicit: "You shall not wrong an alien, or be hard upon him . . . . You shall not ill-treat any widow or fatherless child . . . . If you take your neighbor's cloak in pawn, you shall return it to him by sunset, because it is his only covering. It is the cloak in which he wraps his body; in what else can he sleep? If he appeals to me, I will listen, for I am full of compassion" (Ex. 22:21–27).

The Creation as Grace

GRACE

Meaning

The word *grace* means gift. In Greek it is *charis* from which we get the word charismatic meaning gifted. The Latin is *gratia* from which we get *gratis* meaning free. You do not

An Introduction to Christianity

have to pay for grace; it is not a business transaction. A gift given because I have earned it is not a gift; it is wages. Grace is not wages. A gift given because I deserve it is not a gift; it is my right. Grace, by definition, is undeserved. A gift given because I have been good is not a gift; it is a reward. Grace is not a reward. A gift given with the intention of obligating the recipient is not a gift, it is a political ploy. Grace is not a political ploy. A genuine gift must be given from none of the above motives but only from that form of love we call "generosity," which finds its self-expression in giving.

Response

A gift is also not a gift if it is not received. If I offer you a dollar and you refuse it, I have not given it to you. I still have it and you do not. We have power to nullify the grace of God by refusing it. We sometimes refuse gifts because we distrust the giver; we suspect he is not offering us a gift but a political ploy. More frequently we refuse them from pride. If you refuse my dollar, you will be the poorer for it but you will still have your pride. We do not like to receive gifts because we do not like to think of ourselves as being needy, and we dislike being freeloaders. We sometimes nullify a gift by giving one of equal or greater value in return.

The only appropriate response to grace is gratitude. Grace and gratitude are intimately connected. The Latin *gratia* means both. In Spanish *gracia* is gift and the appropriate response is *gracias* meaning "thank you." The proper response to the Greek *charis* is eucharist meaning "thanks." Gratitude involves humility. For me to be grateful I must perceive something as a gift and receive it as such, that is, as being unearned and undeserved. Some parents breed ingratitude into their children by giving them too large a sense of their own deserving; the parents are later surprised when the children prove ungrateful for what they have learned to regard as their rightful due. Thanksgiving is a kind of giving and is costly to our pride.

We sometimes, correctly, refuse a gift because we do not wish to be in a relationship with the one who makes the offer. For grace and gratitude constitute a relationship. The love from which genuine gifts are given is properly met by love for the giver. *Amor con amor se paga*. (Love is paid with love.) Gifts are tokens of love and thus less important than the giver. To perceive this fact and receive a gift gratefully is to enter into relationship.

Original Grace

Grace is the word we use to denote especially those gifts given us by God. We hear much talk of original sin, but there is original grace as well, namely the creation. The stars and planets, the sun and moon, the earth and sky, the seas, rain, snow, land, trees, plants, animals, the air we breath and water we drink, our very souls and bodies are all gifts from God, unearned and undeserved by us. It is all right that we do not deserve to be here; we do not need to. Being is God's gift to us. One of the most ridiculous phrases in the English language is "self-made man"; man cannot make a mouse, much less himself. We all live from God's welfare; we are all freeloaders. The only difference in this regard between the religious man and the irreligious one is that the former knowingly and gratefully lives by grace and the latter has illusions about himself. If grace is a token of love, what more proof of God's great love for us do we need than the creation itself?

STEWARDSHIP

Gratitude

The religious man stands before the creation with awe, amazement and gratitude. It is paradoxical that gifts are granted but must not be taken for granted else they wither in our hands. If we do not receive the earth as a precious trust and treat it as such, we will pollute it, profane it, and destroy it. The earth is given us for our use but not our ownership, our enjoyment but not our possession. For it shall outlast us; the land we call our own will receive our bones:

For we see that the wise die also;

like the dull and stupid they perish . . . .

Their graves shall be their homes for ever,

their dwelling places from generation to generation,

though they call the lands after their own names. (Ps. 49:10–11)

We must neither take the creation for granted nor hold it in pride of ownership but gratefully receive it for the gift it is.

Property

There was great debate in the last century over who should own what property. Capitalism teaches that we should privately

own whatever we can get our hands on and that we can do
what we like with what belongs to us. Communism teaches
that the people as a whole should own the means of production
so that nobody need be poor. In practice, communism means
that the state owns everything and everybody works for the
government. Communism manages to impoverish the rich
while not enriching the poor. The Biblical view endorses
neither capitalism not communism but stewardship. The Bible
points to neither private ownership nor public ownership but to
divine ownership:

The earth is the Lord's and all that is in it, the world and all
who dwell therein.
For it is he who founded it upon the seas
and made it firm upon the rivers of the deep. (Ps. 24:1–2)
In his hand are the caverns of the earth,
and the heights of the hills are his also.
The sea is his, for he made it,
and his hands have molded the dry land. (Ps. 95:4–5)
Know this: The Lord himself is God;
he himself has made us, and we are his;
we are his people and the sheep of his pasture. (Ps. 100:3)

We find ourselves not in the position of ultimate owners
but of stewards, those who have been entrusted with gifts and
must one day render an account of our management of them.
Not only the nature I understand but the mind I understand
it with, not only the earth I till but the hands I till it with, not

only the air I breathe but the lungs I breathe it with are God's gifts to me, not my own creation but a sacred trust. The ancient Hebrews tithed their produce to God in acknowledgment of its ultimate origin. Faithful people today give a tenth of their earnings to charity in gratitude to the great Giver and in imitation of his graciousness.

Economic Ethics

As we shall see in the next chapter, God has created humans to be co-creators with him. We can take what he has given us and with it earn more than we need. What are we to do with the surplus? John Wesley believed that we should earn all we can, save all we can and give all we can.[10] If I have two coats and see that my brother has none, should I not give my second coat to him? (Lk. 3:11). "Whosoever hath this world's goods and seeth that his brother have need and shutteth up the bowels of compassion from him, how dwelleth the love of God in him?" (I St. Jn. 3:17). Charity cannot be made a matter of secular law else it cease to be charity. The business of the law is justice, not love. But the divine generosity evident in the creation offers us the opportunity to align ourselves with it.

SACRAMENT

Meaning

The entire creation may be regarded as a sacrament. A sacrament is a particular kind of sign. All signs are things that point beyond themselves. I once had a dog named Harry, who was a fundamentalist. We used to play a game in which I would throw a ball and Harry would fetch it. One day he did not see where the ball landed and was running around in circles sniffing for it. Trying to be of help, I began pointing to where the ball lay and shouting, "There it is, Harry. Look there." But instead of looking in the direction I was pointing, the animal ran to me and began eagerly staring at my finger. You cannot understand the point of a sign by looking at the sign; you must look where the sign is directing you. A symbol is a sign that participates in what it points to;[11] it is a vehicle of, as well as a director toward, its meaning. A sacrament is a symbol of the presence of God. Sacraments point beyond themselves to the God who indwells them.

Creation

The entire creation is potentially sacramental. "[T]he soul or spirit of every man in passing through life among familiar things is among supernatural things always, and many things seem to me miraculous which men think nothing of."[12] Each thing that has being participates in Being-Itself. As matter is an embodiment of energy, so physical reality is not anti-spiritual but is an embodiment of spirit making it concrete, here and now. God who is spiritual could have made a purely spiritual creation. But instead of stopping with the angels, he went on to create rocks, rivers, trees, wheat, grapes, water, flesh, breasts, penises, vaginas. How did we ever get the idea that parts of our bodies were dirty? God made them; he loves them. The creation is not only a token of God's love; it is a vehicle of it. God's relationship to his creation could hardly be more intimate; it is an embodiment of divine energy, structured by divine law and held together by divine love. God indwells it as well as transcending it. Any part of the creation can become transparent for its creator, a medium for an encounter with the Holy One.

Idolatry

We should revere but not idolize the creation. An idol is an opaque sacrament. Idolatry results from religious shortsightedness; it comes from focusing upon the gift instead of upon the giver. Things through which we encounter the Holy become themselves holy, for example, a mountain top, a church, a saint, the Bible. They become idols when we cease to understand that their holiness is derivative and secondary. Because our need for incarnation is so great, idolatry is a constant temptation in all religions.

In summary, the creation is from God and can be a means to him. It is an instance of grace and a potential means of grace.

A Song of Creation

Glorify the Lord, all you works of the Lord,
praise him and highly exalt him forever.
In the firmament of his power, glorify the Lord,
praise him and highly exalt him for ever.
Glorify the Lord, you angels and all powers of the Lord,

O heavens and all waters above the heavens.

Sun and moon and stars of the sky, glorify the Lord,

praise him and highly exalt him for ever.

Glorify the Lord, every shower of rain and fall of dew,

all winds and fire and heat.

Winter and summer, glorify the Lord,

praise him and highly exalt him for ever.

Glorify the Lord, O chill and cold, drops of dew and flakes
of snow.

Frost and cold, ice and sleet, glorify the Lord,

praise him and highly exalt him for ever.

Let the earth glorify the Lord, praise him and highly exalt
him for ever.

Glorify the Lord, O mountains and hills,

and all that grows upon the earth,

praise him and highly exalt him for ever.

Glorify the Lord, O springs of water, seas and streams,

O whales and all that move in the waters.

All birds of the air, glorify the Lord,

praise him and highly exalt him for ever.

Glorify the Lord, O beasts of the wild, and all you flocks
and herds.

O men and women everywhere, glorify the Lord,

praise him and highly exalt him for ever.

Let the people of God glorify the Lord,

praise him and highly exalt him forever.

Glorify the Lord, O priests and servants of the Lord,

praise him and highly exalt him for ever.

Glorify the Lord, O spirits and souls of the righteous,

praise him and highly exalt him for ever.

You that are holy and humble of heart, glorify the Lord,

praise him and highly exalt him for ever.

Let us glorify the Lord: Father, Son and Holy Spirit;

praise him and highly exalt him for ever.

In the firmament of his power, glorify the Lord,

praise him and highly exalt him for ever.[13]

IV. Man

What is man that you should be mindful of him? Ps. 8:4

Creature

Man* is the acme of creation, "the measure of all things" except himself.[1] Man is the goal of the evolutionary process; he is what God had in mind all along (cf. Gen. 1:26–30). Having pierced the primeval darkness with light and brought being out of nothingness, having coaxed life from the inorganic slime and having raised instinct to consciousness, how pleased God must have been to have finally evolved a creature with whom he could break bread. What sort of creature is man?

IV. MAN
A. Creature
   1) FINITUDE
   2) HUMILITY
B. Image
   1) THE NAKED APE FALLACY
   2) IMAGO DEI
   3) HUMAN NATURE
     (a) Virtue
       i. Man Is Creative
       ii. Man Is Social
       iii. Man Is Free
     (b) Natural Law
     (c) Righteousness
C. Sin
   1) FALL
     (a) Pride
     (b) Decadence
     (c) Concupscience
   2) ORIGINAL SIN
   3) ACTUAL SIN
     (a) The Terror of Human Freedom
     (b) The Power of Sin
     (c) Why Doesn't God...?

FINITUDE

We are creatures, the work of a higher hand than our own. We cannot make a man and have only limited ability to repair

---

* The word *man* is used throughout the book in its inclusive sense of *Homo sapiens*.

one. Our lives are bound about by many limits. Our life span is limited. "The days of our age are threescore years and ten; and though men be so strong that they come to fourscore years, yet is their strength then but labor and sorrow, so soon passeth it away, and we are gone" (Ps. 90:10 KJV). We are sometimes amazed by the fish kills that result from minute increases in the salinity or temperature of water. Is not the spectrum of our survival but little broader? If the earth were a few thousand miles closer to the sun, we would burn up; if it were a few thousand miles farther away, we would freeze. We would die long before the temperature reached the point at which water boils, and long before it plummeted to absolute zero. If the thermostat in my room were set five degrees higher, I would be uncomfortably warm; if set five degrees lower, I would be uncomfortably cold. We cannot descend to the depths of the sea without shells to protect us from the crushing pressure there; we cannot climb the highest mountains without oxygen tanks to compensate for the inadequate air pressure. Our capacities are limited. No amount of training will enable a sprinter to outrun a cheetah. The brightest polymath will know only a fraction of what is to be known. Human suffering soon overwhelms our capacity for compassion; one man's death saddens me; the murder of six million Jews is unimaginable.

Our physical needs are limited. I have an urgent need for air, but only for so much of it. I cannot breathe twice as much air as you; you do not need four times more air than I do. If you had it, what would you do with it? Try to breathe four times faster to use it all up? We all need a certain amount of food in order to survive, but we can only eat so much. Do you need four times more food than I do? I would be very unhappy if I lacked food, shelter, clothing and transportation, the things that money can buy. But suppose I have all that, and am still not happy? What then? I make a great mistake if I conclude that what I need is more of the same. If I go out and buy a second set of everything so that I now have two houses, two cars, twice as many clothes and twice as much food, will I be twice as happy?

As finite, fleshly creatures, our lives are intrinsically insecure. We are always only a tire-screech away from death. It makes sense to be prudent, to eat right, sleep right, exercise and stop smoking. It makes sense to have a lock on the door, to avoid walking in dangerous parts of the city alone at night and to maintain a police force and armed forces. But, having done all that, we are still insecure. If you have four locks on your door, you will not be four times more secure than I who have one. If you own five firearms you will not be five times more secure than I who have none; you may be less secure because a very unfortunate accident is waiting to happen in your house. Many years ago, we acquired the ability to blow up every city in the Soviet Union. But that was not good enough. We did not feel secure. So we kept building more bombs. Now we can destroy them ten times over. Are we ten times more secure? Are we secure at all? "There is no king that can be saved by a mighty army; a strong man is not delivered by his great strength. The horse is a vain hope for deliverance; for all its strength it cannot save" (Ps. 33:15f).

HUMILITY

A chill went through my bones when a priest first smudged ashes upon my forehead on Ash Wednesday and said, "Remember O man that thou art dust and unto dust shalt thou return." He was right of course. The word *Adam* means man but literally "from the earth." So, too, the word *humility* is derived from *humus*, earth. Humility does not mean breast-beating or low-rating myself; it certainly does not mean a pretense of modesty. Humility is an accurate perception of my limitations. I am only human. I make mistakes; I trip sometimes; occasionally I fall on my face. My knowledge is limited; my energy is limited; my virtue is limited; my ability to love is limited. Humility also means a graceful acceptance of my place in the great scheme of things. I am no longer a young man, and that is all right. I am not yet an elder; that is all right also. I am not an angel; I am not God; I am not a dog, either. I am a man. That is what I was meant to be. I need not try to be God: I need only be the best man I can be. I need not try to be Christ; God already has a Christ; what he wants now is a Sam Todd.

Humility is simply knowing and accepting the truth. Humiliation is learning the truth the hard way; it is having knowledge of our limitations imposed upon us from without; it is being put in our place. Humble people rarely get humiliated. The people who get humiliated are people who have illusions about themselves or pretensions above themselves. Being proven wrong is humiliating only to the know-it-all.

Our finitude is not a problem for two reasons. The first is that a problem has a solution. If it does not have a solution, it is not a problem; it is a fact of life. Problems are to be solved; facts of life, to be accepted. Our finitude is a fact of life. Secondly, God made us finite; it was what he had in mind for us. I need never be ashamed of the way God made me. If he is pleased with the way I am, I am content to live from his estimation of me.

Image

THE NAKED APE FALLACY

Our membership in the animal kingdom is indisputable. But the animal kingdom is not our lost kingdom. Like the lower animals, we must eat, sleep, defecate, copulate and die. There is nothing wrong with any of that, but that is not all we need. The apes and we seem to have descended from a common ancestor. But the key to our nature is not found in what we have come from, but in what we have come for; not in our material cause, but in our final (teleological) one. It is a great mistake to define man only in terms of what is less than man. The macho version of this mistake was prevalent among my high school crowd who sought their self-esteem in their physical strength and beauty, their prowess in fighting and fornicating. But I can hardly prove my manhood by doing what the dogs and cats do. The scientific version of this mistake is to define us merely as a variant animal. Man is the sapient species of the genus Homo of the family Hominidae of the Primate Order of the

Mammal Class of the Sub-phylum Vertebrata of the Phylum Chordata; an animal for whom childbirth is difficult because of a ridiculously enlarged skull; an animal built to walk on four legs, who long ago insisted upon walking erect, and has been having back problems ever since; and the tool-making animal or the weapon-making animal or The Naked Ape.[2] Man "contains a sufficient amount of phosphorous to equip two thousand match-heads, enough sulfur to rid oneself of one's fleas."[3] This last remark circulated in pre-Nazi Germany. Is it such a long step from that to making people into cakes of soap?

Socrates made a perilous career of asking after man's *arete*, his distinctive excellence.[4] The Roman word was *virtus* from the Latin *vir* meaning man. Surely human virtue is to be sought in what distinguishes us from the lower creation. Man is self-transcendent. Never having lived at a time when the world was not, man yet imagined such a time. The creation was given him from the beginning, but man did not take it for granted. He stood before it in awe, wonder and gratitude. Man is the most successful predator of all time, yet he is the only one that feels guilt for killing, passes laws against murder, and sets aside land for a wildlife refuge. Throughout man's history, the present has almost always in some sense been an improvement over the past. Nevertheless, there has persisted throughout every culture and religion the memory of a lost kingdom. Eden turns out to have been a never-never land; our pre-historic habitat was not paradise, but the African veldt. Whence then this memory? The memory is not historical, but ontological. The place of unrealized virtue is not a land in the depths of time but a level in the depths of the human soul. We are faced not with a past forfeiture but with a present possibility. The image that tantalizes us is not that of Adam, but the *imago Dei*, the image of God in which we are made.

IMAGO DEI

Then God said, "Let us make man in our image and likeness to rule the fish in the sea, the birds of heaven, the cattle, all wild animals on earth, and the reptiles that crawl upon the earth. So God created man in his own image; in the image of God he created him; male and female he created them" (Gen. 1:26–27).

Obviously, the invisible God has not created us as literal look-alikes. What Scripture means is that what is most human about us is what we share, not with the lower creation, but with our Creator, namely our spiritual nature. We receive our lower life from God, and it is good as far as it goes. However, we share our higher life with him; for he is spirit. Our spiritual lives are compounded of four dimensions—cognitive, ethical, aesthetic and affective.

It is because of the cognitive dimension of our spiritual lives that we have a thirst for knowledge as well as water. The ambitious mind of man attempts to comprehend the scope of the universe and tries to peer within the nucleus of the atom. We study and write books about cats; they do not write books about us. If truth is the accurate apprehension of reality, then all truth is of God since he is the author of all reality. And since he himself is Ultimate Reality, our thirst for truth should lead us at last to him.

The ethical dimension of our spiritual nature cares about good and evil, and attempts to discern right actions from wrong ones. The physical force we exercise through military might differs only in degree from the lead wolf's intimidation of the pack. But no other animal than ourselves will oppose another's ambition with the stricture, "What you do is wrong!" Our ethical sense differs in kind from anything to be found within the mind of a wolf.

The aesthetic dimension of our spiritual nature is exhibited in the fact that man is the only creature who appreciates and produces beauty, or even has a notion of it. And the thing to note about those we account of lesser taste than ourselves who produce or buy banal art is that they think it beautiful. They have a sense of beauty; they differ in degree from us, but differ in kind from the dogs and cats.

No such sharp distinction can be drawn between ourselves and the lower animals with respect to the affective dimension of our spirituality; for our God, who is love, has distributed this capacity as far down the evolutionary scale as is possible. The lower animals often exhibit a touching affection and tender regard for their mates and offspring. But they do not love those outside their class, let alone another species. Only man becomes or patronizes a veterinarian. And only one man, so rooted in God that it is difficult to distinguish his human from divine being, proclaimed, "Love your enemies, bless them that curse you, do good to them that hate you . . . . That ye may be the children of your Father which is in heaven: for he maketh his sun to rise on the evil and on the good, and sendeth his rain on the just and on the unjust" (Mt. 5:44–45 KJV).

We share with creatures beneath us our physical hunger, sexual desire, thirst, anger, pleasure and pain. We share with God above us our capacity for truth, goodness, beauty and love.

HUMAN NATURE

Man is a composite creature, having both physical and spiritual aspects to his nature. Both are good, both created by God, the latter shared with God.

Virtue

If we look for man's distinctive excellence, we may point not only to his spiritual nature in general, but also to three specific virtues:

—Man Is Creative

Art, music, poetry, dance, sculpture, architecture all testify to our kinship with our creator. Other animals dance; only man choreographs. Other animals communicate; only man writes fiction. Beavers build dams; perhaps we differ from them only in degree in building palaces and temples. But we differ from them in kind in our ability to create out of nothing. Shakespeare's Prospero may have been underscoring our finitude in saying

Our revels now are ended. These our actors,
As I foretold you, were all spirits and
Are melted into air, into thin air;

And, like the baseless fabric of this vision,
The cloud-capp'd towers, the gorgeous palaces,
The solemn temples, the great globe itself,
Yea, all which it inherit, shall dissolve,
And, like this insubstantial pageant faded,
Leave not a rack behind. We are such stuff
As dreams are made on, and our little life
Is rounded with a sleep.[5]

But the opposite point could be made, namely that as God created this earth and Shakespeare himself out of nothing, so the fecund Shakespearean imagination summoned countless countries and characters out of nothing. It is Shakespeare's creativity, not his mortality, that is virtuous.

—Man Is Social

"In the image of God he created him; male and female he created them" (Gen. 1:27). The Holy Trinity, itself a society, created us for society. It is no individual man or woman who bears the image of God, but the two bound together in love who bear the image. Out of the debris of broken marriages, we have tried to turn our failures in love into virtues and much nonsense has been written recently about the wholeness of the single person. We are supposed to feel guilty for needing each other, ashamed to depend upon anyone. If our parents had felt that way, we would not be here. We were created for society, made for each other. We are not created whole, but with the capacity for becoming so through love. I have never known a friendless person who had a gift for friendship but chose isolation instead. It is from lack of social skill, or the courage to risk again our hearts, that we wind up alone. Isolation is by default, not by choice.

Wolves mate for life, and ants are social in their totalitarian way. Only man has a need and capacity for society with God. There is depth to our souls, mysterious even to ourselves, which no psychiatrist can plumb nor human lover fulfill. We have within us an infinite longing that some folk focus upon an infinite and disappointing succession of finite lovers. But our infinite longing is a longing for the infinite. We have within us a God-sized hole that only God can fill. Our created nature is a God-specific love potion. "Thou hast made us for thyself," St. Augustine prayed; "and our souls are restless until they find their rest in thee."[6]

—Man Is Free

"Man is essentially a freedom-event. As established by God, and in his very nature, he is unfinished. He freely determines his own everlasting nature and bears ultimate responsibility for it."[7] Man is the end-point of creation, but his own end-point is undetermined. We are not genetically different from the Cro-Magnon men who painted the Altamira caves some 30,000 years ago. How different our lives are from theirs! Our evolution is now cultural rather than biological, spiritual rather than physical. A sign to be seen in some offices reads: "Have patience. God is not finished with me yet." We can say "yes" or "no" to whatever plans God has for us. "No" was almost the first word my children learned. If you have ever tried feeding strained peas to an infant who really did not want to eat them, you know that human freedom begins very early. We can nullify the grace of God or cooperate with it.

Freedom is the ability to make genuine choices. Migratory birds appear to be navigational wizards, and are; they navigate by instinct. The reason they always make the right choices is that they make no choices at all. Human freedom is ultimately not provable; some folks down through the centuries have denied its existence. Oedipus did everything that he could to escape his fate (to kill his father and marry his mother), but he played right into its hands.[8] Luther denied that we are free; he said we are like beasts who will be ridden either by the Devil or Christ.[9] Calvin taught double predestination: before the creation God ordained who would be saved and who eternally damned.[10] Calvin probably thought he was striking a great blow for God's sovereignty. His theology, however, makes all of human history nothing more than God playing a gruesome game with himself. This is sovereignty?

Some psychologists see us as nothing more than complicated stimulus-response mechanisms. Some social commentators see criminal behavior as just a conditioned reflex to the criminal's environment, and thus blame society for the malefactor's misdeeds. None of these dehumanizing scenarios are disprovable, though all fly in the face of common sense. If any of them are true, you need not waste any time over your next decision; it has already been made for you by fate, providence, genes or society.

Tyrants know we are free, and think we ought not to be. "Sometimes it is said that man cannot be trusted with the government of himself. Can he, then, be trusted with the government of others? Or have we found angels in the forms of kings to govern him? Let history answer this question."[11] Freedom is so basic a human virtue that millions of people have willingly shed their blood to acquire or preserve it for their fellows.

We are certainly influenced by our environment and our freedom is finite. We can build wings but not grow them. I am free to drink gasoline, but not with impunity. I am free to act in many ways, but all those ways have consequences. My freedom would be puny indeed if my actions made no difference, had no consequences.

In summary, human nature is physical and spiritual. In many ways continuous with the lower creation, it has an affinity for its creator as well, particularly in its creativity, sociability and freedom. Human nature gives us a ground for ethics. We have an objective criterion for deciding what is good: that is desirable which makes us more humane, which edifies the cognitive, ethical, aesthetic and affective dimensions of that spirituality which is our distinctive excellence. We must know the nature of a species before we can know whether an individual within it is good or bad. The nature of a knife is to cut; therefore a good knife is sharp, and a dull knife is a bad knife. What is a good man? A good man, by definition, is a virtuous man, a humane man, one who is creative, sociable and free. The "ought" must be grounded in the "is," or it is ungrounded altogether. What is the good life? How ought I to live? So live that your existence actualizes your essence.

In other words, become who God intended you to be; become who you essentially are. Become yourself.

Natural Law

Our nature acts as a law upon us, which we violate at our peril. My body was made by God in such a way that it is nourished by water but not by gasoline. I am free to drink gasoline if I will, but I am not free not to be poisoned by doing so. If I punish my body, I will be punished by it. I cannot violate my nature without killing myself. Since God created my nature, one could say he is the ultimate judge, the dispenser of reward and punishment.

The revealed law is natural law that we did not figure out on our own. God, who created our nature, reveals to us what appertains to our welfare:

> I am the Lord your God who brought you out of Egypt, out of the land of slavery. You shall have no other god to set against me. You shall not make a carved image for yourself . . . . You shall not make wrong use of the name of the Lord your God . . . . Remember to keep the sabbath day holy. You have six days to labor and do all your work. But the seventh day is a sabbath of the Lord your God; that day you shall not do any work . . . . Honor your father and your mother . . . . You shall not commit murder. You shall not commit adultery. You shall not steal. You shall not give false evidence against your neighbor. You shall not covet . . . (Ex. 20:2–17).

God prohibits our having any other gods but him because there are none. He prohibits idolatry not because he is conceited but because he knows idolatry does not work. He is our supreme good. To worship as divine that which is not is to chase after vacuity and become finally vacuous. The Lord once lamented our idolatry in these words: "Two sins have my people committed: they have forsaken me, a spring of living water, and they have hewn out for themselves cisterns, cracked cisterns that can hold no water" (Jer. 2:13). A fellow could die of thirst that way. God forbids our invoking his name when we do not really mean it, because to do so is both to delude ourselves and to play games with ultimate reality; both courses end with a crash. He forbids our working seven days a week because he does not intend us to be beasts of burden; workaholics are in flight from their spirituality, that is, their humanity. It does not take a great deal of intelligence to perceive that the fabric of society will not hold up very well if riven by filial disrespect, murder, adultery, theft, perjury and avarice. Those who wish to see for themselves are getting to do so today.

Righteousness

Righteousness is the condition of being right with reality, that is, with God and with our own nature. The revealed law is not unreasonable. God wills our welfare.

> The commandment that I lay on you this day is not too difficult for you, it is not too remote. It is not in heaven, that you should say, "Who will go up to heaven to fetch it and tell it to us, so that we can keep it?" Nor is it beyond the sea, that you should say, "Who will cross the sea for us to fetch it and tell it to us, so that we can keep it?" It is

a thing very near to you, upon your lips and in your heart ready to be kept. Today I offer you the choice of life and good, or death and evil (Dt. 30:11–15).

Righteousness is usually not too complicated. Professors of ethics like to tease their students by posing ethical dilemmas such as, "whom do you save if your wife and mother are both drowning and you can save only one?" And it is certainly true that we are sometimes faced with a choice between two evils. But most of the trouble most of us get into does not stem from not being able to discern what is right, but from knowing it and ignoring it, or from never even having asked the question.

The path to righteousness begins by asking the right question. Before making an ethical decision, or perhaps more tellingly, before making a political decision, or perhaps more tellingly still, before making an economic decision, ask yourself the question, "Is it right?" Not "Is it expedient?" Not "Is it advantageous?" Not "Will it feel good?" But "Is it right?" The answer may be inconvenient; but the willingness to ask the question, and to act upon the answer, distinguishes us from the dogs and cats.

Moreover, what is right is what will ultimately make us feel good. Human nature is such that happiness is attained not by seeking it, but by seeking righteousness. "Happy are those who hunger and thirst to see right prevail; they shall be satisfied" (Mt. 5:6). Phillips Brooks paints the opposite picture, namely of those who have never thirsted after righteousness. At death, he says, they are all transported into an entirely new realm:

All previous judgements go for nothing unless they find their confirmation there. Men who have been the pets and favorites of society, and of the populace and of their own self-esteem, the change that death has made to them is that they have been compelled to face another standard and to feel its unfamiliar awfulness. Just think of it. A man who, never in his life since he was a child, has ever once asked himself about any action, any plan of his, is this right? Suddenly, when he is dead, behold, he finds himself in a new world, where that is the only question about everything. His old questions as to whether a thing was comfortable, or was popular, or was profitable, are all gone .... And upon the amazed soul, from every side, there pours this new, strange, searching question: "Is it right?"[12]

Sin

FALL

Sin is a falling away from human nature. It is man's proud but futile attempt to be more than human, or his cowardly and successful attempt to be less than human.

Pride

The proud form of sin is a rebellion against our finitude. Pride is the opposite of humility (which is an accurate perception and gracious acceptance of one's proper place in the great scheme of things). The pride that is sinful entails an inaccurate perception of one's proper place and is intrinsically false pride, which is to be distinguished from appropriate pride. If I create beauty in a wasteland, that is proper cause for pride. If I use my intelligence to add to the store of human knowledge, that is proper cause for pride. If by industry I increase my wealth to my own betterment and that of others, I may legitimately take pride. If by dint of determination I turn my frail body into a robust one, I can appropriately take pride in my accomplishment. But if I am born extraordinarily beautiful, intelligent, wealthy or robust, that is cause for gratitude not pride.

False pride often involves pretense. A thirst for knowledge is part of the glory of our spiritual nature; the prideful person pretends to know more than he does. A bane of every teacher's task is the prideful student who, not realizing that his ignorance is the presupposition of his being a student, refuses to ask questions about what he does not know from fear of appearing stupid. Thus the student remains ignorant. Those who pretend to a health they do not have deprive themselves of the medical help they need. Those who pretend to a righteousness they do not have deprive themselves of salvation. When asked why he ate and drank with tax-gatherers and sinners, Jesus replied, "It is not the healthy that need a doctor but the sick; I have not come to invite virtuous people, but to call sinners to repentance" (Lk. 5:31).

Those who do not perceive their proper place deceive themselves. Those who do not accept their proper place become arrogant, little gods. These folk take as their rightful due what belongs to them and what belongs to you as well. These are they who "keep no law and do not fear God" (Ps. 55:19) and "who grind the destitute and plunder the humble" (Amos 8:4). The ordinary thief and rapist we condemn; about the robber barons and those who rape the land and pollute the waters, we feel ambivalent; the great conquerors of history we tend to admire. God scorns them all; "he breaks the spirit of princes, and strikes terror in the kings of the earth" (Ps. 76:12). Pride goeth before a fall:

I met a traveler from an antique land
Who said: Two vast and trunkless legs of stone
Stand in the desert. Near them, on the sand,
Half sunk, a shattered visage lies, whose frown
And wrinkled lip, and sneer of cold command,
Tell that the sculptor well those passions read
Which yet survive, stamped on these lifeless things,
The hand that mocked them, and the heart that fed:
And on the pedestal these words appear:
"My name is Ozymandias, king of kings:
Look on my works, ye Mighty, and despair!"
Nothing beside remains. Round the decay
Of that colossal wreck, boundless and bare
The lone and level sands stretch far away.[13]

Decadence

Another form of sin is to be less than human, to imitate the brutes, to shy away from becoming, to stumble back toward the nothingness from which we have emerged. Heroism will always be ridiculed in an age that sees heroism as beyond its grasp. The jellyfish of our time float along the surface of life believing in nothing, committed to nothing, standing for nothing, accountable for nothing, formless, insubstantial, behaving as the fog behaves, oozing from one situation to another, from one superficial relationship to another, oozing through life. Decadence is renunciation of spirituality, numbing one's mind with drugs, one's awareness with soporifics, salving one's soul with mere creature comforts: a warm meal, a warm bed, a warm body alongside. Decadence is eating, sleeping, copulating and defecating one's way through life with no thought of nobility, no concern for the good, the true and the beautiful.

Concupiscence

St. Augustine said that all sin is misdirected love, concupiscence; and both pride and decadence are forms of it. We have been created with a natural eros for God, who is the source of our spirit and the life of our soul. Our love for him is inbuilt, inescapable and infinite. The promiscuous man or woman is in love with God and does not know it. In directing an infinite longing for the infinite to an infinite succession of finite lovers, one is doomed to disappointment. We have been created with a physical hunger for physical food, and with a spiritual hunger for God. Physical bread will satisfy our physical hunger, which is modest, but not our spiritual need, which is immense. Someone has said that God's love will not put food in our stomachs. That is not true, since God's love provides the bountiful earth. What is true is that putting food in our stomachs will not make us loved. And those who try to feel loved by putting food in their stomachs simply get fat and still feel unloved. The man who owns three Cadillacs is not attempting to solve a physical need for transportation; he is attempting to meet his spiritual need for self-worth. He is saying to the world, "Hey, look at me; look at what I own. This must mean that I am a great guy right? Right? Right?" Wrong. It means that he does not know where to go to get what he needs. Lust, gluttony and avarice are forms of concupiscence. The things of this earth are good in themselves but become junk food if used to satisfy our hunger for God. "Do not labor for the food which perishes, but for the food which endures to eternal life" (Jn. 6:27). If I feed my soul on what does not nourish it, not only do I remain unsatisfied, it becomes malnourished and dies. If God is the life of the soul, it cannot live long without him.

Directing spiritual need to physical objects can also kill others. When predators other than man have satisfied their physical hunger, they stop. Man does not. The mosquito only takes his belly full; he does not put my blood in a bank.[14] If Hitler had been successful, one wonders where he would have stopped. Would Russia have satisfied him? The Middle East? India? The world? It is the unlimited nature of our need for God that makes it so deadly when perverted to physical greed. It is our spiritual endowment that makes our greed so deadly in another way also. A lion with unlimited greed could decimate the local zebra population; he could not commit genocide. Woe betide us all when our higher nature is put into the service of our lower one. The human mind that can peer into the atomic structure of the creation is also able to build atomic bombs to destroy it. Evil is parasitic in that it depends upon good for its effectiveness. It was the genius, industry and organization of the German people that made Nazi malevolence so destructive. If Hitler had won, Europe would have been plunged, as Churchill said, "into the abyss of a new Dark Age made more sinister, and perhaps more protracted, by the lights of perverted science."[15] All sin is a perversion of human nature—reaching beyond our station or falling below it, a need for God directed instead to his handiwork, enlisting our God-likeness in the service of the brute within us.

ORIGINAL SIN

Human folly and perversion have been so universal that our fathers in the faith sought to trace them back to a primeval catastrophe that twisted human nature in its infancy. The Biblical version of this attempt is found in the third chapter of Genesis, the story of Adam's disobedience. St. Paul located Adam's act as the point where sin and death entered the world.[16] St. Augustine later said that Adam's rebellion somehow damaged his genetic material, so to speak, such that his progeny, the whole human race, is born with a deformed nature rather than the nature God made.[17] We are born with concupiscence rather than eros for God. From our very origin we have a clouded intellect, so that we fail to see God as our supreme good; and we have a defective will, so that we cannot act upon the good even when we see it. John Calvin later went so far as to say that we are totally depraved; that is, we have no original righteousness left in us at all.[18] This was a bit much, surely. If we were totally depraved, we would not know there was anything wrong with us.

But the primary flaw in the traditional notion of original sin is that its validity depends upon the historicity of the Genesis creation account. But the account is not historical. There was no first man named Adam who ate the forbidden fruit. More to the point, traditional notions of original sin assume that man has fallen from a past perfect state, and we know the contrary to be the case. There was never a time when we were as we should be, never a time when we were better than we now are. There certainly was a time—all time prior to the present century—when we were less destructive than we now are, but that was due to ignorance, not virtue. Our actual progenitor was Australopithecus, not Adam.[19] The human pilgrimage has been a long trek from savagery and barbarism. Our problem is not that we are worse than we used to be but that we are little better than we used to be.

Real original sin is an evolutionary lag. We still carry within ourselves the seeds of those predatory apes that were our ancestors. Primitive instincts, conjoined to modern technology can spell our doom. When we feel threatened, even just psychologically, our bodies begin the changes necessary to prepare us for fight or flight. Since it is in poor taste to do either, we get ulcers instead. But the man with a weapon in his hand—or worse, "the button"—need not get ulcers.

ACTUAL SIN

The Terror of Human Freedom

"What is horrible is not the beast but the man who has become a beast," Nicolas Berdyaev wrote.[20] Our predatory past gives us a tendency to grab what we want and attack what stands in our way. The evolutionary lag tugs us toward being destructive

instead of creative, selfish instead of social, instinctual instead
of free, brutal instead of godlike. But we do not have to be so.
The tendency to sin becomes actual sin only when acted upon
by a person free to do otherwise. Who has to steal? Most theft
is done not by the poorest but by the least scrupulous.

Most of the evil we lay at God's door is of human origin. Does
God write bad checks? Get drunk and run over children? Take
from the mouth of labor the bread it has earned? Build bombs?
Set up torture chambers? Run Auschwitz? I once asked Rabbi
Abraham Heschel if the holocaust had destroyed his faith in God.
He said not but that it had almost destroyed his faith in man.[21]

The Power of Sin

We do not have to sin, but each sin makes the next more
likely. The second theft, murder, act of adultery is easier than
the first. The voice of conscience, overridden by will, grows
weaker. Then the will itself, grown accustomed, habituated,
addicted to sin, grows weak. An act begets a habit; a habit
begets a character; a character begets a destiny. The secret act
of self-indulgence, which served us once so well, becomes
master. The once daring sinner becomes the creature of sin,
its plaything, its slave. In misusing our freedom, we lose it,
becoming less than human, a monstrosity alienated from God,
from our neighbors, from our essential selves:

> I discover this principle then: that when I want to
> do the right, only the wrong is within my reach. In my
> inmost self I delight in the law of God, but I perceive that
> there is in my bodily members a different law, fighting

against the law that my reason approves and making me a
prisoner of the law that is in my members, the law of sin.
Miserable creature that I am, who is there to rescue me
out of this body doomed to death? (Rms. 7:21–24).

Why Doesn't God ... ?

The stars keep to their spheres, and the sun knows the time
of its setting.[22] All creatures obey God's laws, save man. Cubs
grow into full lions, and dogs become all that they were meant
to be. Only man falls short of his essential nature:

> Hark you heavens, and earth give ear, for the Lord has spoken:
> I have sons whom I reared and brought up,
> but they have rebelled against me.
> The ox knows its owner and the ass its master's stall;
> But Israel, my own people,
> has no knowledge, no discernment (Isa. 1:2–3).

What is God to do? The question cannot be why he does not
make us better than we are. To make us better (More placid?
Cow-like?) would remove our freedom. To evolve a creature
with consciousness is to make one who is aware of alternatives
and thus can act upon them. There is no spirituality without
consciousness, no consciousness without freedom. Without
freedom, we would not be human. So the question is not why
God did not make us better than we are, but why he made us at
all. As the creator who made and continues to make human evil

possible, God must bear ultimate responsibility for it. What is he to do about it?

Why, having made us and seen the results, does he not disintegrate his creation? When people ask, "How can God allow a world like this?" they are really asking, "How can God tolerate creatures like us?" Many people think God had the right idea in Noah's day:

> "If I were as our Lord God," cried Luther in his vivid way, "and these vile people were as disobedient as they now be, I would knock the world in pieces." . . . He being what He is, we being what we are, why He does not shrink back from us in shuddering loathing, or blast us into annihilation as an affront He cannot have in the same universe with Himself—that is very difficult to understand. And is there any explanation except that suggested to us by, say, such a passage as that remarkable chapter Ecclus. 43, in which the writer loses himself among the immensities of the heavens, and wanders stunned and dazed amid the mysteries of creation—so vast, so many, so unthinkable—while, suddenly, stabbingly, there comes the tremendous thought, "As is His majesty, so also is His mercy" (Ecclus. 2:18). The divine is all upon that absolutely superhuman scale. God Himself is love: a love that utterly breaks through our human conceptions of what love means and is; and runs out to lengths that sound incredible to our human ears, because no man could do it.[23]

God does not need to destroy us. We can do that ourselves. The question is, can he save us?

V. Christ

When in former times God spoke to our forefathers, he spoke in fragmentary and varied fashion through the prophets. But in this the final age he has spoken to us in the Son whom he has made heir to the whole universe, and through whom he created all orders of existence: the Son who is the effulgence of God's splendor and the stamp of God's very being, and sustains the universe by his word of power. When he had brought about the purgation of sins, he took his seat at the right hand of Majesty on high . . . . Hebs. 1:1–3

V. CHRIST
A. Incarnates God's Love
　1) GOD'S PURPOSE
　2) OUR NEED
　3) JESUS CHRIST
B. Teaches God's Love
　1) GOD'S LOVE
　　(a) The Good News
　　(b) The Loving Father
　　(c) Our Response
　2) LOVE OF NEIGHBOR
　　(a) Mercy
　　(b) Forgiveness
　3) THE GREAT EQUIVALENCE
C. Ministers God's Love
　1) THE CONFLICT WITH SATAN
　　(a) Exorcising Demons
　　(b) Healing the Sick
　　(c) Forgiving the Sinful
　2) THE CONFLICT WITH THE PHARISEES
　3) THE CONFLICT WITH ROME
D. The New Creation

Incarnates God's Love

GOD'S PURPOSE

"Love (*eros*) then . . . is the desire for the perpetual possession of the good."[1] God is our supreme good, in relationship to whom alone our lives find purpose, order and fulfillment. But are we God's good? Can he desire us? The Greeks thought not. To them God was, by definition, perfect, complete, wanting nothing. This presupposition largely prevailed in Christian theology. But the Greek portrait of the perfect God, eternally content to contemplate himself, ill accords with the Biblical experience of the God who, throughout the Old Testament, rants and raves like a jealous lover at each instance of his people's idolatry. Is so much fulmination to be ascribed purely to his disinterested devotion to our welfare (*agape*)? Were a few philosophers right, and so many prophets wrong? Perhaps the difference in perspective is because the Greeks were not the chosen people. Thus, their idolatries were merely errors, not infidelities. God revealed himself to various peoples in various ways. The Greeks were most perceptive in discerning the rational order of creation. But it was not they whom God chose to be the entering wedge of his covenantal relationship with humanity. Why was it the Hebrews? Why this insignificant race of Semitic nomads? Perhaps to emphasize that election is by grace, not by merit. Or perhaps they were simply the first people to listen; Abraham, the first son to obey.

If my son flunks out of school, it is, in one sense, no skin off my nose, since I will still have my diploma. If he dies, I will still be here. My children's misdeeds and misfortunes do not diminish me—unless I love them. Then they break my heart. Compassion is the willingness and ability, perhaps the necessity, to feel what someone else is feeling, of suffering with him if need be. Another word for it is *mercy*, another is *love*. Does God need us? We may say at least this much: "It pleaseth him in his mercy to account himself incomplete and maimed without us."[2]

From the beginning, God sought not just to create, but to make the creation itself creative; not just to know, but to be known by it; not just to unify his creation, but to evolve within it a creature with whom he could unite, to engender a creature in whom he could be engendered. After light had pierced the darkness and being had been brought forth from nothingness, after eons of evolution had culminated in man, after a people had been called who heard and revered the divine word, finally, in the fullness of time, the inconceivable God was conceived; and he, whom the highest heavens cannot contain, yielded himself to lie within the confines of Mary's womb, there to fashion for himself arms of flesh with which to embrace us.

OUR NEED

We are not content merely to live; we wish to live meaningfully. We want our religion to be relevant to our daily round of activities. But what is the relevance of our daily round? Do we go merely round and round, or do we proceed toward some end? We know that our workaday lives come to an end, though we know not when. But if we knew our end, what then? That would not be to know for what end our end. A period is not a purpose, a finale not fulfillment. We have many ends and contrive many means to reach them. But even in so doing we sense that all our ends and means are meaningless without that End for the sake of which all our ends are merely means.

Even while repeating Freud's refrain that life is desire, satisfaction, desire, satisfaction, we remain dissatisfied with satisfaction. For we know our desires to be ephemeral, and we desire permanence. We exploit nature to satisfy our needs, while remaining frustrated that nature cannot satisfy the deepest need of our nature, which is to be needed. Is there a need in the universe for us?

We seek meaning. Some philosophers assure us that the quest for meaning is meaningless, because meaning is a human invention. But the quest for meaning is the motive for reasoning. Surely it is absurd to label as unreasonable the precondition of reasoning. We suspect that man is a meaningful invention.[3] But whose?

Even as we make bold to equate reality with availability, reducing the realm of "what is" to the province of "what can be measured and manipulated," we yet long to become instruments of that immeasurable, which we cannot manipulate but only appreciate. But what is it?

We are aware of our problem, but such awareness is itself problematic, since the solution remains dark. Never before have we been so lucid about our blindness. Yet such lucidity does not restore sight. What does?

To place the label "God" upon what we do not know does not, in the final analysis, enlighten us. Our ignorance, labeled, remains ignorance. We want not an answer but a response. We need not a name but a personal address. We ask not for the pseudo-knowledge of nametags but for intimacy with our Father. He is our origin and aim. He has made us for himself, and our souls are restless until they find their rest in him.[4] But where can we find him?

We know from science that our universe and all within it is permeated by empty space. We sense in faith that the universe is suffused with the presence of the Most High. But how can we come within the presence of the Presence? Can the first and the last become present to us? We need the Alpha and the Omega to be right here and now. It is not comprehension we seek; we know well enough that God cannot be comprehended, only adored. We ask for guidance to a place we might come and adore him.

At Christmas a star leads us to the place of the Presence. Our question is answered, our longing fulfilled. The great gift of Christmas is a child born for us, a son given to us. Our own presents given and received are but tokens of God's presence in our flesh, Emmanuel. And, when we meet our maker on the other shore, will not his first question to us be, "Did you ever receive the gift I sent you?"

In the Incarnation, God bestows upon us the gift of sight: the light that enlightens everyone has come into the world. We sense that our lives are a garbled articulation of the divine; in Christ we meet the very Word of God.[5] He is the self-expression of the inexpressible. At Christmas, the ineffable receives a personal name—Jesus.

JESUS CHRIST

He is like us in all respects save sin. Like us, he grew tired (Jn. 4:6); he hungered (Mk. 11:12); he thirsted (Jn. 19:28). Like us he could be racially provincial (Mt. 15:26) and make erroneous statements (Mk. 9:1). I feel sure that, like us, he woke with a full bladder and sometimes an erection. We have come to so despise our humanity that some pious heretics would strip Christ of his. Galileo showed us that we are not at the center of the universe; Darwin told us that we are descended from apes; Freud showed that we are a lot less rational than we thought we were; and Hitler demonstrated to us just how thin is the veneer of civilization. We know our kinship with the lower creation; Christ demonstrates what we have in common with the Creator. He is the exemplar of humanity, revealing our essential magnificence. God and man are not intrinsically inimical; they belong together. Humanity and divinity are not essentially incompatible; the Incarnation could not have happened if they were. So Christ shows us something about ourselves we very much need to know.

He also shows us much about God we could never have guessed. The God revealed in Christ is not at all as we would have designed divinity. We would build palaces for ourselves; God is born into the world in a barn at Bethlehem and is placed in a manger. We are anxious for security; God in Christ abandons himself to our mercy. We regard comfort as an inalienable right; he is born into discomfort and denies himself. While we are hungry for status, he empties himself and assumes the form of a servant. We, like Herod, are avid for power and will sometimes kill to acquire it; God in Christ is determined to share his power with us and will die to do it. Knowing that neediness is not attractive, we strike poses of independence. Christ is love triumphant over majesty. God comes to call us with our own voice and wanders the Galilean hills, living off the land and the charity of women.

In the one person, Jesus Christ, is forged the union that both God and man desire. He is consubstantial with the Father and with the children of Eve. His face is full of the glory of God, yet he is flesh of our flesh and bone of our bone. Gregory of Nazianzus wrote:

> He dwelt in the womb—but He was recognized by the prophet, himself still in the womb, leaping before the Word, for whose sake he came into being. He was wrapped in swaddling clothes—but he took off the swathing bands of the grave by his rising again. He was baptized as man—but he remitted sins as God. He hungered—but he fed thousands; yea, he is the bread that gives life, and that of heaven. He thirsted—but he cried, "If any man thirst, let him come unto me and drink." He was wearied, but he is the rest of them that are weary and heavy-laden. He weeps, but he causes tears to cease. He is sold and very cheap, for it is only for thirty pieces of silver; but he redeems the world, and that at a great price, for the price was his own blood. As a lamb he is silent, yet he is the Word, and is proclaimed by the voice of one crying in the wilderness. He is given vinegar to drink mingled with gall. Who? He who turned the water into wine, who is the destroyer of the bitter taste, who is sweetness and altogether desired . . . . The veil is rent, for the mysterious doors of heaven are opened; the rocks are cleft; the dead arise. His inferior nature, the humanity, became God . . . because it was united to God, and became one person because the higher nature prevailed . . . in order that I too might be made God so far as He is made man.[6]

Teaches God's Love

GOD'S LOVE

The Good News

He was of obscure birth and parentage. He came from an area of the country that even Israelites regarded as provincial. Presumably, he assisted his father in the family carpentry business; but, when he was about thirty years old, he went to the Jordan River to hear a prophet named John and was there baptized by him. After John had been arrested for denouncing the ruler's violation of the law, "Jesus came into Galilee proclaiming the gospel of God: 'The time has come; the kingdom of God is upon you; repent and believe the Gospel'" (Mk. 1:14f). The word *gospel* means good news. Jesus' good news was that the longed-for event was happening: God was reclaiming his authority from those who had usurped it. Again, as in the time of the Exodus, the Lord was acting to liberate his people from bondage. The sphere of God's renewed dominion began small but would grow to the size of an empire. "It is like a mustard-seed which a man took and sowed in his garden; and it grew to be a tree and the birds came to roost among its branches" (Lk. 13:19). It looked small but would exert enormous influence. "It is like the yeast which a woman took and mixed with half a hundredweight of flour till it was all leavened" (Lk. 13:21).

Who deserves to enter the Kingdom of God? The righteous: "I tell you that unless your righteousness exceeds that of the scribes and Pharisees, you shall not enter the Kingdom of

Heaven" (Mt. 5:20). Who are the righteous? Those who keep the Law: "Anyone who keeps the Law, and teaches others so, will stand high in the kingdom of Heaven" (Mt. 5:19). What Law? Jewish law was composed of what we would call ritual laws and moral laws. The former had to do with diet, ablutions, sacrifices and that sort of thing. The latter regulated people's relationships with each other. Jesus dispensed with the ritual laws as being of human invention (Mk. 7:8). About diet he said, "nothing that goes into a man from outside can defile him; no, it is the things that come out of him that defile a man" (Mk. 7:15). About the sacrifices, he reminded the Pharisees of the text, "I require mercy not sacrifice" (Mt. 12:7; 9:13, cf. Hosea 6:6). The moral law, on the other hand, Jesus made more stringent in his Sermon on the Mount, so much loved and so little kept by generations since:

You have learned that our forefathers were told, "Do not commit murder . . . ." But what I tell you is this: Anyone who nurses anger against his brother must be brought to judgement . . . . You have learned that they were told, "Do not commit adultery." But what I tell you is this: If a man looks on a woman with a lustful eye, he has already committed adultery with her in his heart . . . . Again, you have learned that our forefathers were told, "Do not break your oath" . . . . But what I tell you is this: You are not to swear at all . . . . You have learned that they were told, "Eye for eye, tooth for tooth." But what I tell you is this: Do not set yourself against the man who wrongs you. If someone slaps you on the right cheek, turn and offer him your left (Mt. 5:21f, 27f, 33f, 38f).

Jesus' thrust throughout the Sermon on the Mount is to go through the action to the motive behind it and to demand righteousness in our hearts as well as in our deeds. He also thrusts through the commandment to the divine intention behind it (cf. Mk. 10:4–5). Having stripped away the externals, Jesus places us face to face and heart to heart with God himself. Indeed, the justification for Jesus' demands is the nature and activity of God:

> You have learned that they were told, "Love your neighbour, hate your enemy." But what I tell you is this: Love your enemies and pray for your persecutors; only so can you be children of your heavenly Father, who makes his sun rise on good and bad alike, and sends the rain on the honest and the dishonest . . . . And if you greet only your brothers, what is there extraordinary about that? Even the heathen do as much. There must be no limit to your goodness, as your heavenly Father's goodness knows no bounds (Mt. 5:43–48).

The very thing some people point to as evidence of God's injustice—namely, that he does not destroy the wicked—Jesus points to as evidence of his great generosity and would have us imitate it.

If righteousness is as Jesus describes it in the Sermon on the Mount, who is righteous? Very few. Perhaps no one. Then who deserves entrance into the kingdom of God? Very few. Perhaps no one. But generosity is the quality of giving more than is deserved. "Fear not, little flock; for it is your Father's good pleasure to give you the Kingdom," Jesus tells his disciples (Lk.

12:32). Elsewhere, Jesus compares the Kingdom to a landowner who went out early in the morning and hired laborers to work in his vineyard for the usual day's wage. As the day wore on, he went out three more times, the last an hour before sunset, and hired more laborers. At sunset, he paid them all a full day's wage. The laborers first hired were outraged that those coming at the eleventh hour received as much as they. The owner said, "My friend, I am not being unfair to you. You agreed on the usual wage for the day, did you not? Take your pay and go home. I choose to pay the last man the same as you. Surely I am free to do what I like with my own money. Why be jealous because I am kind?" (Mt. 20:1–15). Grace is always inequitable because it goes beyond our deserving. Whether grace is good news or bad may depend upon our sense of our own deserving.

The Loving Father

One reason we call Jesus the Son of God is that he seems to have been the first person in human history to call God "Father." Israel regarded God as father of the nation, but their favorite form of address to him was "Lord God." Kings occasionally called God "Father" in a formal way, as a means of asserting that they wielded his authority. But Jesus seems to have used the intimate "Abba" (Daddy) in speaking to or about God. The word connotes the spontaneous affection of a young child for a father he trusts unreservedly. Jesus is speaking out of his relationship with God, not claiming an ontological status. Moreover, Jesus taught us to call God "Father": "In your prayers do not go babbling on like the heathen who imagine that the more they say the more likely they are to be heard. Do not imitate them. Your Father knows what your needs are before you ask him. This is how you should pray: 'Our Father in heaven . . .'" (Mt. 6:7–9).

But the world is full of fathers, some of whom are terrible. What sort of father is God? Jesus has told us. What follows is his story with my reflections upon it:

> A certain man had two sons: And the younger of them said to his father, "Father, give me the portion of goods that falleth to me." And he divided unto them his living. And not many days after the younger son gathered all together, and took his journey into a far country, and there wasted his substance with riotous living.

When we want to leave him, our heavenly Father lets us go. To do otherwise would deprive us of our freedom, and God will never do that. If we insist on doing it on our own, he will allow us to do it on our own. He will allow us to wound him and ruin ourselves, rather than take away our freedom. He would rather we hate him than not love him freely.

> And when he had spent all, there arose a mighty famine in that land; and he began to be in want.

What he did with his freedom was not very imaginative or very wise. He simply wished to enjoy his freedom but wound up depleting his substance and found himself empty. The substance God gives us is not money but life. God's life and love are the source of our lives and our happiness. When we run off from him, we have run away from our only sources of fulfillment. Then we, like the prodigal son, are embarrassed, have to put a good face on it, lie to everyone, and pretend that we are very happy, thank you. Did you ever run away from home and then begin wondering what to do as night fell and your stomach began rumbling?

> And he went and joined himself to a citizen of that country; and he sent him into his fields to feed swine. And he would fain have filled his belly with the husks that the swine did eat: and no man gave unto him.

In what he thought to be the interest of his freedom, the prodigal underwent a transition from sonship to serfdom. He was worse than a slave, even worse than dead in Jewish eyes because he lived among pigs, the vilest animals imaginable. He journeyed from life to death. Having deserted our Father in heaven in order to be free, how many temporal lords do we find ourselves subservient to, tyrants who lack any compassion for us? Success in business is a hard taskmaster; it has no use for failures. Beauty is an unforgiving queen; she has not much use for us when the wrinkles start appearing. Wit and charm are lords quick to laugh at us when we make fools of ourselves. What tyrant do we serve, trying desperately to earn the life and love our heavenly Father gave us for free?

> And when he came to himself, he said, "How many hired servants of my father's have bread enough and to spare, and I perish with hunger!" I will arise and go to my father, and will say unto him, "Father, I have sinned against heaven, and before thee. And am no more worthy to be called thy son; make me as one of thy hired servants."

"[H]e came to himself . . . ." God is not only in heaven but also within each of us. His image is as much part of us as are our hands, heart and stomach. God's image within calls to God without. To come to ourselves is to come to our Father. "I will arise and go to my father"—the son overcame the one thing that kept him mired in misery: his false pride. The Greek word for arise is *anastasis*, the same word we translate resurrection. The dead son was about to be resurrected. He was not a great sinner; few of us are. He was not a murderer or a thief or a cruel person. He was simply a prideful person, as most of us are. The death of that false pride enabled him to arise. Put another way, his repentance put him on the road to reconciliation. Repentance means to get up, turn around and head for home.

The son returned to his father, not in triumph as he might have wished, but as a penitent. But how will his father receive him? Will he receive him back at all, no matter how much the son humbles himself? Possibly the father will forgive him after a period of probation. We now come to the heart of the parable, in which Jesus reveals the heart of God.

> And he arose, and came to his father. But when he was yet a great way off, his father saw him, and had compassion, and ran, and fell on his neck, and kissed him. And the son said unto him, "Father, I have sinned against heaven, and in thy sight, and am no more worthy to be called thy son." But the father said to his servants, "Bring forth the best robe, and put it on him; and put a ring on his hand, and shoes on his feet: And bring hither

the fatted calf, and kill it; and let us eat, and be merry: For this my son was dead, and is alive again; he was lost, and is found." And they began to be merry.

Have you ever lost a child? A few years ago, on a Colorado mountain ten thousand feet high, I became separated from my two youngest children, both girls. I had sat down for a breather, and they had pushed on. When I went to catch up with them, they had disappeared. For two hours I searched for them, to no avail. Over and over again I shouted their names and listened intently for any sound save the wind. I wept. I prayed. Finally, in fear and sadness, I began to descend the mountain to fetch the police. Halfway down, I saw the girls traipsing merrily along. I cannot describe my sense of relief and of sudden, miraculous reprieve. This is the very experience Christ chooses to convey our Father's response when we return to him: "For this my son was dead, and is alive again; he was lost, and is found."

How foolish and embarrassed the prodigal must have felt, bedraggled, grimy and guilty as he was, to be made to stand and be adorned with sandals and a ring. How incongruous the beautiful robe must have felt. Yet it is the robe and ring, not the grime and guilt, that represent the prodigal's true identity; for he is a son, not a slave.

Christ adds to the parable the story of the elder brother's reaction, perhaps to contrast God's response to the sinner with that of those who account themselves righteous and love to stoke the fires of hell for the wicked.

Now his elder brother was in the field: and as he came and drew nigh to the house, he heard musick and dancing. And he called one of the servants, and asked what these things meant. And he said unto him, "Thy brother is come; and thy father hath killed the fatted calf, because he hath received him safe and sound." And he was angry, and would not go in: therefore came his father out, and intreated him. And he answering said to *his* father, "Lo, these many years do I serve thee, neither transgressed I at any time thy commandment: and yet thou never gavest me a kid, that I might make merry with my friends: But as soon as this thy son was come, who hath devoured thy living with harlots, thou hast killed for him the fatted calf."

The elder brother is bitter and resentful. We understand his reaction because it is completely understandable; it is human. He is a legalist. But the law has not been broken. The elder son will inherit the estate. The younger son is not given a new inheritance; that is gone forever. What the younger son receives is his father and the restoration of their relationship. The grace occurs within the law; the elder brother, who has always done the right thing, and has the estate, lacks grace. He does not refer to his younger brother as "brother," but as "thy son." He does not call his father "father." The elder brother has everything save love. He has neither a father nor a brother for company, only his own rectitude. He has missed the point. His pride is undented. He will fall into no one's arms; no one will embrace him. He receives the prodigal as perhaps the prodigal deserved. But God does not so receive us. There is no reproach in his heart, only joy at our return.

And he said unto him, "Son, thou art ever with me, and all that I have is thine. It was meet that we should make merry, and be glad: for this thy brother was dead, and is alive again; and was lost, and is found (Lk. 15:11–32 KJV).

Forgiveness is the highest form of love, because it is love that maintains itself in the face of rejection and injury, that is, in the face of an enemy. People think that forgiveness of enemies is very radical, but it is only our enemies we can forgive. God's love goes the length of forgiveness. He would rather restore a relationship than stand upon his righteousness.

Our response

Jesus tells us that we can count on God's love. We may rely upon it. To do so is what he means by the word *faith*. We are saved or not saved by whatever we rely upon to save us. Jesus speaks so often of money because that is what most of us most rely upon. But how long is it worth something? Jesus told the story of the man who stockpiled wealth for himself and relied upon it. "But God said to him, 'You fool, this very night you must surrender your life; you have made your money—who will get it now?' That is how it is with the man who amasses wealth for himself and remains a pauper in the sight of God" (Lk. 12:20f). "Do not store up for yourselves treasure on earth, where it grows rusty and moth-eaten . . . . Store up treasure in heaven where there is no moth . . ." (Mt. 6:19f). "You cannot serve God and Money" (Mt. 6:24). "How little faith you have! No, do not ask anxiously, 'What are we to eat? What are we to drink? What shall we wear?' All these are things for the heathen to run after, not for you, because your heavenly Father knows you need them all. Set your mind on God's kingdom and his justice before everything else, and all the rest will come to you as well" (Mt. 6:31–33). Relying upon our Father's love for us, we should ask him for whatever we need. "Is there a man among you who will offer his son a stone when he asks for bread, or a snake when he asks for fish? If you, then, bad as you are, know how to give your children what is good for them, how much more will your heavenly Father give good things to those who ask him!" (Mt. 7:9–11).

The kingdom of God is so magnificent that it is like a pearl of great price or a treasure buried in a field, for whose purchase a man would be willing to sell everything he has (cf. Mt. 13:44–46). We may trust God so completely that we may sell our belongings and rely upon his sustenance. "Have no fear little flock; for your Father has chosen to give you the Kingdom. Sell your possessions and give in charity. Provide for yourselves . . . never-failing treasure in heaven . . . . For where your treasure is, there will your heart be also" (Lk. 12:32–34). Did Jesus really believe all this? Yes; he acted upon it. No one ever trusted God's love more than Jesus did.

LOVE OF NEIGHBOR

"'Master, which is the greatest commandment in the Law?' [Jesus] answered, 'Love the Lord your God with all your heart, with all your soul and with all your mind.' That is the greatest commandment. It comes first. The second is like it: 'Love your neighbour as yourself.' Everything in the Law and the Prophets hangs on these two commandments" (Mt. 22:36–40).

Mercy

One day a lawyer came forward to test Jesus. He was not a lawyer of the secular Roman code, but of the Law of Moses, which intricately regulated affairs among Israelites. The law seeks to ensure justice, i.e., that each person receives his due. Justice is all we can ask of anyone, and it is the least we should give. The lawyer asked a deeper-than-legal question: "Master, what must I do to inherit eternal life?" Jesus referred him back to the Law and asked his reading of it. The lawyer replied with the summary of the Law quoted above. "'That is the right answer,' said Jesus; 'do that and you will live'" (Lk. 10:28).

But the lawyer "wanted to vindicate himself"; so he then asked, "And who is my neighbor?" This is a legal question; its purpose is to ascertain the limits of his obligation. Jesus replied by telling a story about what it means to be a neighbor: A man (presumably a Jew) was on his way to Jericho when thieves stripped him, beat him, and left him for dead. A priest came along but passed by on the other side. Nothing illegal here; indeed, the priest would have profaned himself by touching a dead body. A Levite (sort of a layreader) also came by and did not stop. The Law prohibits inflicting injury but does not require one to help. Then came a Samaritan, one of a people despised by the Jews because they espoused a heretical variant of Judaism. No self-respecting Jew would hold converse with a Samaritan. But when the Samaritan saw the ravaged Jew, he "was moved to pity" (Lk. 10:33). None of us want pity until we stand in dire need of it. The Samaritan bound up the Jew's wounds, took him to an inn, and paid the innkeeper. "Which of the three," Jesus asked, "do you think was neighbour to the man who fell into the hands of the robbers?" "The one who had showed him kindness," the lawyer replied. Jesus said, "Go and do as he did" (Lk. 10: 36–37). Do what? Be merciful? Mercy is what we ask for when we are caught dead to rights. Mercy goes beyond justice. Is it now to be a legal requirement? This would undermine the Law altogether.

Forgiveness

In the Sermon on the Mount, Jesus invoked the example of God himself in urging us to love our enemies and pray for our persecutors (cf. Mt. 5:43–48). To illustrate his point more vividly, Jesus told the story of a king who called to account a servant who owed him millions. As the man could not pay, the king ordered him, his family and possessions to be sold to pay the debt. "'Be patient with me,' he said, 'and I will pay in full'; and the master was so moved with pity that he let the man go and remitted the debt." As soon as the servant went out, he saw another servant who owed him a few dollars. Seizing him by the throat, the first servant demanded payment. "The man fell at his fellow-servant's feet, and begged him, 'Be patient with me and I will pay you'; but he refused and had him jailed until he should pay the debt." When the king heard of it, he was outraged and had the unforgiving servant brought before him.

"'You scoundrel!' he said to him; 'I remitted the whole of your debt when you appealed to me; were you not bound to show your fellow-servant the same pity as I showed you?' And so angry was the master that he condemned the man to torture until he should pay the debt in full. And that is how my heavenly Father will deal with you, unless you each forgive your brother from your hearts" (Mt. 18:23–35).

Jesus prefaced the story by saying, "The kingdom of Heaven, therefore should be thought of in this way" (Mt. 18:23). In other words, there is an economy of forgiveness in God's kingdom. On the one hand, he has forgiven us, and we should therefore forgive each other. On the other hand, in the end, God will forgive us as we have forgiven others. "For if you forgive others the wrongs they have done, your heavenly Father will also forgive you; but if you do not forgive others, then the wrongs you have done will not be forgiven by your Father" (Mt. 6:14–15, cf. Mk. 11:26).

But if forgiveness is to be the law, what becomes of the Law? How is it to be enforced? And what sanctions do we retain in the face of our enemies when we pray daily, as Jesus taught us, "Forgive us the wrong we have done, as we have forgiven those who have wronged us" (Mt. 6:12, cf. Lk. 11:4)? Are we to be disarmed?

THE GREAT EQUIVALENCE

Jesus has spoken of God's love for us and urged us to rely upon it. He has spoken in radical terms of what our love for our neighbor entails. But what of our love for God, whom we are to love with all our heart, all our soul, and with all our mind? What does love of God entail?

Love of God will certainly entail that we seek him out directly in prayer. Jesus' ministry is punctuated by prayer. Verses like the following are scattered throughout the Gospel narratives: "And after he had dismissed the crowds, he went up on the mountain by himself to pray" (Mt. 14:23, cf. Mt. 19:13; 26:36; Mk. 6:46; 14:32; Lk. 6:12; 9:28; Jn.17). Jesus also urged the disciples to pray (Mt. 5:44; 24:20; 26:41; Mk. 13:18; 14:38; Lk. 6:28; 11:2; 18:1), and he taught them how to pray (Mt. 6:5–9; Lk. 10:2).

The relationship with God that Jesus invited people to, and urged upon them, is nurtured in prayer. But it is exhibited in action. Jesus says of himself: "I do as the Father commanded me so that the world may know that I love the Father" (Jn. 14:31). He criticized the Pharisees because they "neglect justice and the love of God" (Lk. 1:42). In other words, love of God entails that we obey his will, that we not only pray "thy kingdom come, thy will be done" but also act accordingly.

What does God will? That we should go to church, bring sacrifices to the temple? Jesus points us to the text "I require mercy, not sacrifice" (Mt. 12:7). He says "If, when you are bringing your gift to the altar, you suddenly remember that your brother has a grievance against you, leave your gift where it is before the altar. First go and make your peace with your brother, and only then come back and offer your gift" (Mt. 5:23f). In other words, when we come to adore God, he points us back to our neighbor.

God's will is our welfare. God gave the Law, not so he could watch us jump through hoops, but to guide us to what appertains to our welfare. "The Sabbath was made for the sake of man and not man for the Sabbath" (Mk. 2:27).

Love entails not only feeling but also practical action. What love for God entails, Jesus tells us very plainly in the picture he paints of the Last Judgment. All nations will be arrayed before the king, who will separate them into two groups as a shepherd separates the sheep from the goats.

> Then the king will say to those on his right hand, "You have my Father's blessing; come, enter and possess the kingdom that has been ready for you since the world was made. For when I was hungry, you gave me food; when thirsty, you gave me drink; when I was a stranger you took me into your home, when naked you clothed me; when I was ill you came to my help, when in prison you visited me." Then the righteous will reply, "Lord, when was it that we saw you hungry and fed you, or thirsty and gave you drink, a stranger and took you home, or naked and clothed you? When did we see you ill or in prison, and come to visit you?" And the king will answer, "I tell you this: anything you did for one of my brothers here, however humble, you did for me" (Mt. 25:34–40).

The righteous are not judged righteous on the basis of their prayer life, their pledge to the church, their attendance at worship, their study of the Bible, or their having accepted Jesus as their Lord and Savior. The righteous are deemed righteous on the basis of no law save that of love. Their love of God is judged solely by their love of neighbor, any neighbor. Their love of neighbor is judged solely by their having had mercy upon him. Their mercy is judged solely by their actions.

Ministers God's Love

Jesus embarked on an imperative mission of divine love to redeem what love had created. God's redemptive love was not an abstraction; it was incarnate in Jesus of Nazareth and directed to specific people within the mentality and circumstances of first-century Palestine. Christ's mission met opposition from those who would keep others enslaved. The story of his ministry is the story of a power conflict.

CONFLICT WITH SATAN

We have seen that sin is more than human ill will; it acquires power over us. It is superhuman in the sense that it is systemic. It can corrupt a society, deforming its institutions and culture. It can corrupt a person's soul, mind, and body, robbing him of integrity. The sinner, like the alcoholic, is both actor and victim of his disease. In first-century Palestine, the power of sin was personified in the figure of Satan.

Satan is the adversary of God and man, attempting to thwart God's intention by destroying his human creation. Satan is the tempter who offers a drink to the alcoholic and a chance to play double-or-nothing to the compulsive gambler. He is well acquainted with the characteristic weakness of each of us and meets us there. He whispers to us, "Of course you will not die. God knows that as soon as you eat it, your eyes will be opened and you will be like gods" (Gen. 3:4f). He is the sponsor of vice, making the destructive look attractive. He presents adultery as exciting, fidelity as boring. War is offered as a stirring test of manhood, appeasement as craven. Satan is the father of lies. He whipsaws us by telling us one moment that we shall be like gods and telling us the next moment that we are just garbage and might as well commit suicide. The lie most commonly believed is the heresy of perfectionism, namely, that I can and should do all things perfectly, else I am a failure. Evil, like cancer, is parasitic; it has no being of its own but is the corruption of a created good. (Christ, putting being and doing in their proper order, urged us to be perfect, that is, to be fully human [Mt. 5:48]. We may then regard with relaxed humility the successes and failures of our actions.) Satan's greatest lie is that he is all-powerful and God, weak or non-existent. Many good people acquiesce in evil around them and become compliant with it, out of cowardice and the misapprehension that goodness is futile, that evil rules the world.

After his baptism, Jesus, reversing Adam's situation and fall, was placed in a desert, and there was tempted as severely as any of us are. But he did not give in to the tempter, did not lose faith in God (Mt. 4:1–11). Adam was placed in a paradise but craved the one thing forbidden him because it would make him "like gods" (Gen. 3:5). Jesus was placed in a desert and refused the tempter's offer of food and power (Mt. 4:4, 10); though tempted, he refused to tempt God (Mt. 4:7). By his obedience, humility, privation and suffering, Jesus won for us the victory that Adam lost. The campaign that culminated in the cross began in the desert. Then, full of the Holy Spirit, he began contradicting Satan's lie, by proclaiming the good news: "The kingdom of God is upon you" (Mk. 1:15). But is God's kingdom powerful? And if so, what sort of power does the Lord wield?

Exorcising Demons

It is impossible to discern from a twenty-first-century perspective just what the demoniacs' problems were, how we would diagnose them today. It is clear that they were severely alienated from themselves and society. And, like those whom we today call psychotics, they often could not distinguish their sickness from themselves. A cure could seem at first like dying. Jesus' encounter with the demons often began with a poor soul's cry: "Have mercy on me, Son of David!" (e.g., Mt. 15:22; 17:15). Jesus commanded the demons to depart, and they did. What did his cure actually consist of? One cannot really order darkness out; one dispels it by letting light in. Love is the power that overcomes alienation. We cannot say by what combination of spiritual shock treatment and encouragement to the soul curled up inside the sickness Jesus was successful. What is clear is that he restored the possessed to their right minds and rightful Lord.

Healing the Sick

The term *psychosomatic* attests our modern reapprehension of the wholeness of persons. It is not so easy as we once thought to sort out psychic (psyche is Greek for soul) from physical problems. We know there are foreign bodies—viruses, microbes, pathogens—that get into us and make us sick. We also know that not everyone exposed to pathogens becomes ill. Our spiritual vitality and general physical health have much to do with our resistance to disease. Not only can anxiety not add a foot to our height, as Jesus pointed out (Mt. 6:27), it can shorten our lives, and give us colitis in the meantime.

First-century folk were also aware that illness could be caused by foreign agents or internal disarray, or both. The former they called demons, and the latter, sin. God's redemptive love, incarnate in Christ, overcame both. The cure often began in response to that same desperate cry: "Jesus, Son of David, have mercy on me!" (cf. Mk. 10:47; Mt. 9:27; 20:30; Lk. 17:13, 38). Did Jesus really perform healing miracles? The word *miracle* is from the Latin *mirari* meaning "to wonder at." So the miraculous has much to do with our capacity for wonder. I find my daughter Miranda wonderful. Jesus certainly healed people. The healings are too numerously attested for some not to have happened. Even Jesus' enemies did not deny the healings took place; they just attributed them to Satanic power (odd theology). Jesus characteristically told the recipients of his grace, "Thy faith hath made thee whole" (cf. Mt. 9:22, 29; 15:28; Mk. 5:34; 10:52; Lk. 7:50; 8:48; 17:19; 18:42).

Forgiving the Sinful

Jesus did not go around tooting his own horn, claiming to be the Christ; his purpose was to point us to the Father and reclaim us for him. But Jesus implicitly asserted a wide-ranging authority of his own. Though he lacked human credentials (he was not a priest, not a scribe or lawyer, not a licensed rabbi), he presumed, in the Sermon on the Mount and elsewhere, to redefine the Mosaic Law. He also broke the Law in the interest of mercy, healing people on the Sabbath, for example (Mt. 12:1–14). He presumed to speak the mind and will of God purely on his own authority.

The greatest authority Jesus asserted was the authority to forgive sins. St. Mark tells us of the time Jesus was teaching in someone's home in Capernaum, and a paralyzed man was brought into the room. "Jesus . . . said to the paralyzed man, 'My son, your sins are forgiven.' Now there were some lawyers sitting there and they thought to themselves, 'Why does this fellow talk like that? This is blasphemy! Who but God alone can forgive sins?'" (Mk. 2:5ff). Precisely the point.

St. Luke tells us that when Jesus was dining at the home of a Pharisee named Simon a woman who "was living an immoral life in the town" came into the room. She fell at Jesus' feet, weeping, and began wiping her tears off his feet with her hair and anointing his feet with expensive oil. Simon said to himself that if Jesus were a real prophet he would know the woman was a sinner and would not allow her to touch him. But Jesus said to Simon, "'I tell you, her great love proves that her many sins have been forgiven; where little has been forgiven, little love is shown.' Then he said to her, 'Your sins are forgiven.' The other guests began to ask themselves, 'Who is this, that he can forgive sins?'" (Lk. 7:36–50).

St. John describes Jesus teaching in the Jerusalem temple and the doctors of the law and the Pharisees dragging before him a woman:

> Making her stand out in the middle, they said to him "Master, this woman was caught in the very act of adultery. In the Law Moses has laid down that such women are to be stoned. What do you say about it?" They put the question as a test, hoping to frame a charge against him. Jesus bent down and wrote with his finger on the ground. When they continued to press their question he sat up straight and said, "That one of you who is faultless shall throw the first stone." Then once again he bent down and wrote on the ground. When they heard what he said, one by one they went away, the eldest first; and Jesus was left alone with the woman still standing there. Jesus again sat up and said to the woman, "Where are they? Has no one condemned you?" She answered, "No one, sir." Jesus said, "Nor do I condemn you. You may go; do not sin again" (Jn. 8:4–11).

The Pharisees managed to frame a charge against him anyway. The charge was blasphemy.

CONFLICT WITH THE PHARISEES

In addition to scandalizing the Pharisees by acting like God, Jesus raised the issue: Is this the way God acts? The Pharisees thought not. As far as they were concerned, God had given the Law and was now stuck with it. They considered the Law an all-sufficient catalogue of obligations between God and the people of God, and between one person and another. It is true that the Pharisees had hedged the Law about with additional restrictions to ensure that no one came close to trespassing against God's will. But so long as one kept the letter of the Law, he was righteous and could demand that God keep his part of the bargain. Legal righteousness was all that could be required or should be expected of anyone. Those who failed to keep the Law were sinners, to be condemned and avoided.

The problem with the Law, any law, is that it can define righteousness but cannot produce it. It can only condemn the sinner; it cannot redeem him. Jesus saw the Law as God's guidance for our welfare, not as superseding it. Thus he broke the Law on occasion by healing the sick on the Sabbath or picking grain on the Sabbath when he was hungry. His justification was simply: "The Sabbath was made for the sake of man and not man for the Sabbath" (Mk. 2:27). The Law was a gift of God's love, not a substitute for it. The Pharisees had the Law, but had missed the motive behind it. In Jesus' view, keeping the Law was no cause for self-congratulation if one lacked the love that had motivated God's giving it. What made Jesus angry—about the only thing that did—was the Pharisees, the religious authorities, those who spoke in God's name, condemning those whom God meant to redeem. If God had been content to condemn his wayward human creation, he could and would have dissolved it long ago. Jesus' word to the Pharisees was, "Alas, alas for you, lawyers and Pharisees, hypocrites that you are! You shut the door of the kingdom of Heaven in men's faces; you do not enter yourselves, and when others are entering, you stop them" (Mt. 23:13, cf. Mt. 6:2ff; 6:16; 15:7; 22:18).

Shunning the sinful is good policy so long as your only concern is preserving your purity. It does nothing for the sinner, of course, except increase his isolation and despair. Jesus went to the outcasts and invited them in. He even made a disciple out of a tax collector, a type hated even more then than now because they kept for themselves whatever they collected beyond what Rome required. The whole thrust of Jesus' ministry was reclamation of the lost: thus the exorcisms, thus the healings, thus the going out to the despised and dispossessed, and thus many of the parables.

> Another time the tax-gatherers and other bad characters were all crowding in to listen to him; and the Pharisees and the doctors of the law began grumbling among themselves: "This fellow", they said, "welcomes sinners and eats with them." He answered them with this parable: "If one of you has a hundred sheep and loses one of them, does he not leave the ninety-nine in the open pasture and go after the missing one until he has found it? How delighted he is then! He lifts it on to his shoulders, and home he goes to call his friends and neighbours together. 'Rejoice with me!' he cries. 'I have found my lost sheep.' In the same way I tell you, there will be greater joy in heaven over one sinner who repents than over ninety-nine righteous people who do not need to repent" (Lk. 15:1–7).

The Pharisees were not persuaded and began taking counsel how they might destroy Jesus.

Jesus saw the adumbration of his passion and called his disciples together on the eve of the Passover for a last supper. There he interpreted for them the meaning of his ministry and also gave to the Church her internal mission: "I give you a new commandment: love one another; as I have loved you, so you are to love one another. If there is this love among you, then all will know that you are my disciples" (Jn. 13:34f). This is an amazing statement coming from Jesus, because love is so important to him that he almost never used the word. Today there is probably no more debased word in the English language than *love*. Crooned or shouted from a million radios, assiduously exploited by advertisers, even imprinted on a postage stamp, the word has become shabby, dog-eared, almost meaningless. What it frequently does mean is simply "I have the hots for you" or "you make me feel good" or even "it tastes good" (I just love pistachio ice cream). Of course anything precious will be counterfeited. But even within the Church, perhaps especially in the Church, the word has been trivialized. We say "I love you" almost because it would be impolite not to. We say it as almost the equivalent to "have a nice day." Jesus never did this. He talked about love constantly, but almost never spoke the word, as if it were too holy to pronounce, like God's name. He fed the hungry (Mk. 6:35–44); he healed the sick; he preached good news to the poor. But he never once said to anyone, "I love you." And even here, on this last night of his mortal life, among those he had loved most and longest, he preferred actions to words.

Everyone wore sandals in those days and so arrived at a home with dirty feet. If the host had any claim at all to being a gentleman, he would have a servant wash the guests' feet. Turning this convention on its head, Jesus knelt and washed his disciples' feet. This action illustrated something he had told them previously: "You know that in the world, rulers lord it over their subjects, and their great men make them feel the weight of authority; but it shall not be so with you. Among you, whoever wants to be great must be your servant, and whoever wants to be first must be the willing slave of all—like the Son of Man; he did not come to be served, but to serve, and to give up his life as a ransom for many" (Mt. 20:25 ff).

As Jesus used the word love to interpret the meaning of his life, so he used his death to interpret the meaning of the word love. "This is my commandment: love one another as I have loved you. There is no greater love than this, that a man should lay down his life for his friends" (Jn. 15:11–13). Jesus dramatized the meaning of his death yet further when he "took bread, and having said the blessing . . . broke it and gave it to the disciples with the words: 'Take this and eat; this is my body.' Then he took a cup, and having offered thanks to God he gave it to them with the words: 'Drink from it, all of you. For this is my blood, the blood of the covenant, shed for many for the forgiveness of sins'" (Mt. 26:26–28).

There were a number of ways Jesus could have avoided the ordeal before him (run away, recant, change the tenor of his teaching), but all of them involved betraying the mission with which he had been entrusted. Fidelity to the Father required that he go on to the end. In this sense only did God demand Jesus' death. It is absurd to suggest that God needed his pound of flesh from his son Jesus before he was willing to forgive his other children. Christ's entire ministry had been a vehicle of the Father's forgiveness, not a wheedling of it. In the end, Christ chose to offer his life as a sacrifice for the sin that would deprive him of it. He offered blood in atonement for sin in accordance with the Law that would condemn him on the morrow.

Shortly after the Last Supper, the religious authorities arrested Jesus, charged him with blasphemy, and found him guilty—as if it were God who needed protection, and not their theology. But the religious authorities were under the authority of the state authorities and had not themselves authority to put Jesus to death. So they sent him to Pilate.

CONFLICT WITH ROME

The Romans, who invented the word *virtue*, had their own notion of it. The "manly" man, they said, is courageous, just, prudent, sober and, above all, strong. He is a conqueror. The Romans exemplified the virtues they encouraged. This small people, who dwelt in the Alban hills, overthrew Etruscan hegemony, withstood their Samiite neighbors, conquered Italy, conquered Spain, and defeated the Carthaginian Empire in three successive wars. During the Second Punic War, the Carthaginian genius, Hannibal, invaded northern Italy and annihilated three Roman armies sent against him. The Roman response was to raise more armies. Hannibal had counted on help from the client Roman city states, which the Carthaginians had liberated in the north. But the freed cities refused to get involved, not because they loved Rome, but because they feared her. The clients knew that the Romans were still alive within their city walls and that unless Hannibal broke down those walls and extirpated the Romans, root and branch, man, woman and child, they would emerge at last, put down the invader, and deal ruthlessly with those who had collaborated. Which is exactly what they did. The ancient Romans spared neither themselves, nor their property, nor, least of all, their enemies. It was the Romans who finally crossed to north Africa, broke down the walls of Carthage, burnt its buildings, enslaved its populace, and sowed the site with salt. Utter discipline and utter ruthlessness enabled the Romans to go on to conquer Greece and Egypt and Palestine.

Pontius Pilate, a representatiave of Rome, was a civilized society's viceroy sent out to keep order in an unruly and inhospitable land. Back home, the streets were paved, and the buildings built of marble. Here, most roads were dirt, and the buildings made of stucco. The Jews may have regarded their land as promised of God, but, as far as Pilate was concerned, they were welcome to it—except for its strategic significance as the crossroads of Asia and Africa. The reason the Romans had personnel there had nothing to do with the attractiveness of the land or its people.

The people. They were even more difficult than the land. They spoke a language not even cognate with Latin. Their religion was perverse. Rome's religion was sophisticated and tolerant, if cynical. Roman polytheism would acknowledge and incorporate the gods of whatever people the Romans conquered. The subject peoples would in turn acknowledge Jupiter and Juno and burn incense to the Roman Emperor's effigy. This was religion in the service of politics and sophisticated culture. Every subject people understood this and went along with it—except the Jews. Why they did not was difficult for a Roman to understand.

What Pilate could, and did, understand was that the Jews nourished nationalistic ambitions, which they preferred to participation in a worldwide civilization. The Passover was a national, and potentially dangerous, holiday. That is why Pilate had traveled from his normal residence in the Roman-built city of Caesarea Phillipi on the coast to the ancient Jewish capital of Jerusalem for the holiday. And that is why he had brought a lot of Roman soldiers with him. The natives would be restless; trouble could be expected; you just did not know from what quarter it would come.

Neither Holy Scripture nor Roman records have preserved the police blotter statistics for this Passover weekend. We do not know how many riots and barroom brawls Roman soldiers were compelled to quell over the holiday. The only disturbance of record that has survived is that the native religious authorities came knocking at Pilate's door, dragging in tow a compatriot from the provinces whom they accused of blasphemy, and whom they demanded be put to death for his offense. It was surely with dutiful patience and barely concealed exasperation that Pontius Pilate received this delegation from the Sanhedrin and listened to their rantings and ravings. Surely he was about to dismiss the delegation out of hand, perhaps flog the wretched prisoner to appease the mumbo-jumbo witch doctors, and then let the fellow go. But then they accused Jesus of claiming to be a king.

At this, Pilate's boredom vanished. His eyes narrowed; his ears pricked up. This was what he was here for. His whole career, his entire future, depended on how he handled precisely such matters as this. "So you are a king?" he asked (Jn. 18:37).

A king. It is hard for Americans to understand the import of the title or the question. Kings ruled the earth from the kings of Sumeria in 3,700 BC until recent times. Royalty still reigns in England, and Americans flock there and pay to traipse through Buckingham Palace to ogle and sniff the accoutrements of royalty. For want of anything better, we invent and attend our own kings and queens (of the homecoming, the cotillion, the garlic festival, etc.).

Today, whether here or in Britain, kingship has more to do with pageantry, prestige and social cachet than with power. But in most places in most times, kingship has had everything to do with power: political power, power to command, to check, to compel, to raise up and tear down, to enrich and to destroy, to reward and to punish. Pilate had some of it, at the emperor's sufferance. "Knowest thou not that I have power to release thee and power to crucify thee?" he asked Jesus (Jn. 19:10 KJV).

Poor Jesus. He knew of no kingship but God's, of no power save divine love. In the name of that power he had battled demons and disputed with the doctors of the Law. In the name of that power he had forgiven even capital sins (Jn. 7:53–8:11), which the Jews did not expect their Messiah to do. And he had refused to lead a revolt against Rome, which their expected

Messiah would have done. "Pay Caesar what is due to Caesar, and pay God what is due to God," he had said (Mk. 12:17). Not only was he innocent of the Sanhedrin's accusation, but it had condemned him partly for this very reason, i.e., that he had refused to foment an insurrection. Though Jesus was not recognized by the Jews as a conqueror and would not have been recognized by the Romans as one, he was not lacking in the qualities the Romans considered virtuous.

Jesus was courageous. What greater courage could there have been than to leave the only life he had known to embark upon a perilous task for God, to return to his home town on a mission his contemporaries could only have regarded as presumptuous (Mt. 13:54ff), knowingly to have offended the authorities of his religion, to have confronted the merciless machinery of the Roman state without arms, to have calmly withstood Pilate's threat? Behold the man. He did not lack courage; yet he did not preach courage as a virtue, but rather faith in God.

Nor did he lack the prudence of self-discipline or the temperance of sobriety. Though his enemies called him a drunkard (Lk. 7:34), anyone of our overweight population must be impressed by this man who fasted for forty days in the wilderness (Mk. 1:13). Our campers must admire this man who walked the hills of Galilee and forbade his disciples to carry with them a purse or cloak or sandals (Lk. 10:4). His requirements for discipleship may have seemed imprudent, since they militated against his having any disciples at all. And indeed he had none on this final day. Of those men upon whom he had lavished the most love and attention, one betrayed him, one denied him, all deserted him. Behold the man. But he did not preach temperance or prudence as virtues, but rather hope in God.

Jesus was more than just, giving much to many who had no claim upon him (cf. Mt. 15:21–28), and more than was deserved to all. Nor was he lacking in strength; he gave us a new notion of strength. Like the Romans, he was willing to endure unlimited suffering for his cause. Unlike them, he was not willing to inflict suffering on others for his cause. He had the strength of compassion, of healing, of nurturance. He combined what we have been taught to think of as masculine strength with what we regard as feminine strength. He was hard on himself, yet compassionate to the weak. He was strong, yet merciful. He redefined strength for us, and manliness and virtue. He was strong, yet never preached strength as a virtue, but rather love. He had the Roman virtues, and added to them others: faith, hope and love. Behold the man (cf. Jn. 19:5).

Could Pilate claim to be half the man Jesus was? Yet he held the power to release or crucify. The only power Jesus thought significant was God's. To that power he utterly subordinated himself, and in that power he totally trusted. He may even have thought the power of God could or would spare him the unspeakable death that Pilate flicked in his face (cf. Mk. 15:34). But love has no defense against evil.

"So you are a king?" Pilate asked. Anticipating Stalin's question about the pope, he might well have added, "How many legions do you command?" And then Pilate condemned Jesus to crucifixion. To placate a crowd he despised, to cover himself in case of a later Senate investigation, to put down impudence, and because he was tired and had not wanted to come to this provincial city in the first place, Pilate decreed that this man should have spikes driven into his wrists and feet and, thus impaled, helpless, upon crossed beams of wood, should be left to die—from pain, from shock, from thirst, from suffocation, from a broken heart. The man cried out, "My God, my God, why hast thou forsaken me?" (Mk. 15:34 KJV).

The religious authorities, watching the torture, "jested with one another: 'He saved others,' they said, 'but he cannot save himself. Let the Messiah, the King of Israel, come down now from the cross. If we see that we shall believe'" (Mk. 15:31f). They shared their Roman oppressors' definition of power. Jesus' agony was to them but further proof of his God-forsakenness. And, indeed, no one has ever seemed so betrayed by God—not because no one ever died a more painful death, but because no one ever vouchsafed God so much trust to betray.

Those whom Jesus had come to save—the great unwashed, every one in the aggregate whom the Bible calls simply "the crowd," so quick to hail a hero and so quick to turn upon Him—had offered Jesus their despair, and he had preached good news to them; they had offered Jesus their hunger, and he had fed them; they had offered him their sick, and he had healed them; they had offered him their sin, and he had forgiven them. On this day, they offered Jesus their condemnation and ridicule. They cried for the release of the nationalist assassin Barabbas and for Christ's crucifixion. And while he hung on the cross, they jeered him (Mk. 15:29).

Somehow, from the depths of his agony, the man cried out, "Father, forgive them; they know not what they do" (Lk. 23:34). This is the authority Christ does have, the authority to forgive sins (cf. Mk. 2:10). It is why we call him the King of Love.

As an ironic afterthought, Pilate had inscribed on his cross "The King of the Jews" (Mk. 15:26). Thus Rome dealt with claimants to kingship.

Three hundred years later, the sign of that same cross was imprinted upon the brow of the Roman emperor at his coronation. For better than a thousand years thereafter, that same cross was signed upon the forehead of any man who would be king in the western world, after he had knelt and sworn allegiance to Jesus Christ, the King of Kings. Now, two thousand years later, the sign of that cross is imprinted upon the foreheads of millions throughout the world who, through it, receive the highest honor and identity that they will ever have, namely, that they are "sealed by the Holy Spirit in Baptism and marked as Christ's own for ever."[7]

The New Creation

What strange transforming energy imprinted the image of a crucified man on the Shroud of Turin?[8] It is no more strange, really, than the energy compressed in a handful of uranium, which, unlocked, will power a ship for months, or blow us to smithereens in an instant. But though the Shroud has been with us much longer than atomic energy has, it still seems the stranger of the two because it speaks of that singularity when the heavens swooped down like a benign tornado and emptied one tomb of its contents. The resurrection of Jesus Christ is that unique event in human history when eternity bisected time, dividing it forever into before and after.

History does not record Pontius Pilate's reaction when the soldiers brought news to him of the jailbreak at the graveyard. Today, Pilate would classify the report "Top Secret" and begin warming up the paper shredder. And there would have begun dawning upon him the most awful suspicion that he had screwed up. People like Pilate live in perpetual fear of offending the wrong person. The mind that had conceived thermonuclear fusion as a device to power the stars to give light and life to the world, had been standing in front of him. Pilate had squinted at Jesus and asked suspiciously, "Are you some kind of a king?" Something like that. The power that had created matter from absolutely nothing and then patted it into stars and planets and oceans and people had been standing right in front of him. And Governor Pilate, after thinking it over for a few minutes, had given as his considered judgment, "Crucify the bum." Oh well, you can't call them all right.

The religious authorities quickly put about the story that the disciples had come and stolen the body (Mt. 28:11–15). The story is still trotted out from time to time.[9] It is called a cover story.

Some people today are not surprised by the resurrection. The disciples were surely surprised. They did not believe it at first. They saw it and still could not believe it. Some people figure that Jesus was God; so of course he rose from the dead. But they have the cart before the horse. Jesus was a man; he was just as human as you and I. He was a much more faithful man than I certainly, and he did some truly remarkable things. He almost certainly was not aware of himself as the incarnation of the Second Person of the Triune Godhead. And those who knew him best never doubted for a moment that he was human. The only reason the disciples were driven to the conclusion that he must somehow be divine as well as human is that this man, who was as dead as a run-over dog, got up and walked out of the tomb. Doubting Thomas was actually the first person to call Christ "God" (Jn. 20:28). But that was only after, and because, his lord who had been crucified, dead and buried, was suddenly standing in front of him, very much alive. The resurrection is not a doctrine deduced from the general tenets of the Christian faith. On the contrary, the Christian faith is a way of life, and a way of understanding life, wholly derived from the event of the resurrection. If there had been no resurrection, there would have been no Christian faith, no Church, and no New Testament. Sunday would be just another day of the week instead of the first day of the new creation.

Given the first creation, what is miraculous about the new creation is not that it could happen, but that it did. What is truly a marvel is that, when we returned to God the gift of his son, rejected, beaten and dead, he did not simply receive him into his glory and pull the plug on us. The wonder is that Christ came back to those who had deserted him, and not in anger, but holding out his holy, broken hands to them in forgiveness.

"'Peace be with you!' he said, and then showed them his hands and his side. So when the disciples saw the Lord, they were filled with joy. Jesus repeated, 'Peace be with you!' and said, 'As the Father sent me, so I send you.' Then he breathed on them, saying, 'Receive the Holy Spirit!'" (Jn. 20:9–22).

The resurrection gives hint to the whole human race that our future may be open-ended. May be. For we still must speak of how we can so link our lives to Christ's that he pulls us heavenward, how we can begin living his eternal life now, how we can participate in the new creation.

For the moment it is cause enough for joy to know that he who embodied, stood and spoke for the qualities we most admire, the earnest promptings of our deepest nature and our highest aspirations, has risen triumphant over the pettiness and wickedness that always assault them. The courage, honesty, and compassion, the faith, hope and love that cowards and cynics dismiss as naive are of God and are eternal. They shall endure when all the glitter of the world has turned to dust and ashes.

The resurrection means that Pilate's question is answered. Jesus Christ is some kind of king:

King of Kings
Hallelujah! Hallelujah!
And Lord of Lords
Hallelujah! Hallelujah!
And he shall reign for ever and ever.[10]

VI. Church

Give thanks to the Father who has made you fit to share the heritage of God's people in the realm of light. He rescued us from the domain of darkness and brought us away into the kingdom of his dear Son, in whom our release is secured and our sins forgiven. He is the image of the invisible God; his is the primacy over all created things. In him everything in heaven and on earth was created . . . the whole universe has been created through him and for him. And he exists before everything, and all things are held

VI. CHURCH
A. Life in the Spirit
  1) THE HOLY SPIRIT
    (a) The Content of Grace
    (b) Living from Grace: Paul
      i. Paul, the Converted Pharisee
      ii. Paul, the Forgiven Sinner
      iii. Paul, the Inspired Saint
    (c) Discipleship
  2) THE BODY OF CHRIST
    (a) Salvation Is Corporate
    (b) The Church Is the Community
    (c) It Is Christ's Church
  3) THE HOLY CATHOLIC CHURCH
    (a) Her Hypocrisy
    (b) Her Fidelity
    (c) God's Fidelity
B. The Movement Into God
  1) WORSHIP
  2) THE SACRAMENTS
    (a) Embodiments of Grace
    (b) At Christ's Command
      i. Baptism
      ii. The Holy Eucharist
    (c) Other Sacramental Rites
      i. Confirmation
      ii. Marriage
      iii. Reconciliation
      iv. Unction
      v. Holy Orders
  3) SPIRITUALITY
C. The Movement Into the World
  1) EVANGELISM
  2) THE WORKS OF MERCY
  3) HEALING SOCIETY
    (a) Church and State
    (b) Justice
    (c) Mercy

together in him. He is, moreover, the head of the body, the church . . . . Through him God chose to reconcile the whole universe to himself, making peace through the shedding of his blood upon the cross—to reconcile all things, whether on earth or in heaven through him alone.

Col. 1:12–20

Life in the Spirit

THE HOLY SPIRIT

"I will ask the Father, and he will give you another to be your Advocate, who will be with you forever—the Spirit of truth. The world cannot receive him, because the world neither sees him nor knows him; but you know him, because he dwells with you and is in you. I will not leave you bereft; I am coming back to you" (Jn. 14:16–19).

The Content of Grace

I have written previously of the formal character of grace as a free gift. It is now time to open the package and speak of the content of grace. All genuine gifts are tokens of friendship; the friendship itself is the gift behind the gift if we choose to receive it. God has given us many gifts, creation and redemption being chief among them, but the gift behind the gift, for the sake of which the others are given, is eternal friendship with God. In this friendship, each partner retains his own identity; there is no "drop of water returning to the ocean," so to speak. God remains God, and man remains man, but the two are bound together in intimacy by love. Creative love produced us. Redemptive love restored us to relationship with God when we had "wandered far in a land that was waste".[1] Sanctifying love unites us in eternal intimate friendship with God.

An exchange takes place in friendship, an exchange of life. To love a friend is to be open to receive him as he is. It is also to reveal myself to him as I really am and to give myself to him. One who loves God gives his life to God and receives the grace of God. God, who loves man, receives us as we are, with all our sins upon our head. And he reveals himself to us and gives his life to us. Since his life is eternal, to receive God is to receive eternal life now.

The power of grace is mysterious in that it is incomprehensible, that is, we can never wrap our minds around it. It is mysterious in that it is unfathomable; we never get to the bottom of it, never exhaust its depths. But it is not irrational or magic. We have all probably been affected, moved, perhaps changed by the force of someone's personality. There are people so vibrantly alive that their life force impacts all around them. There are people so charismatic that you sense immediately when they have entered the room. There are people so loving that we are drawn to them almost irresistibly. Their love is their personhood reaching out to us. Their life force is not amorphous, but has the form of their personality. God is such a person. To know him is to be transformed by him. His life force has the character of his personality; in fact, it bears an uncanny resemblance to Christ. His love is himself reaching out to us and clasping us to him. The Biblical name of the force of God's personality is "The Holy Spirit."

The Holy Spirit is God's life force affecting, moving, changing people. The Holy Spirit is the power of grace, which, transforms us into the likeness of Christ, making us holy with the wholeness of Christ's humanity united to God. To use an analogy, the Father is the transmitter, we are the receivers, the carrier wave is the Holy Spirit, the message is Christ. It is not that we become Jesus. It is rather that the Holy Spirit conforms us to who Christ would have been, had he become incarnate in the twenty-first-century American you instead of in a first-century Palestinian Jew named Jesus of Nazareth. Christ inaugurates a new humanity united to God; we participate in that humanity through the Holy Spirit:

> For all who are moved by the Spirit of God are sons of God. The Spirit you have received is not a spirit of slavery leading you back into a life of fear, but a Spirit that makes us sons, enabling us to cry, "Abba! Father!" In that cry the Spirit of God joins with our spirit in testifying that we are God's children; and if children, then heirs (Rms. 8: 14–16).

What we are heirs of is eternal life, which we can begin living now. So the Holy Spirit is both the gift and the promise, both the power of grace and the content of it.

Living from Grace: Paul
—Paul, the Converted Pharisee

If one wonders what would have happened to one of the Pharisees if he had ever discarded his self-righteousness and embraced the good news Jesus was trying to give him, one need only study the life and letters of St. Paul. Paul gave us his pedigree: "If anyone thinks to base his claim on externals,

I could make a stronger case for myself: circumcised on my eighth day, Israelite by race, of the tribe of Benjamin, a Hebrew born and bred; in my attitude toward the law, a Pharisee; in pious zeal, a persecutor of the church; in legal rectitude, faultless" (Phil. 3:4–6).

Paul was like the elder brother in the parable of the Prodigal Son. He was typical of those unpleasant persons with whom Jesus argued in the gospels. Righteousness was by the book. He kept the letter of the law; so he was righteous. If you didn't, you weren't, and Paul wouldn't let you forget it. The gospel of grace so infuriated him that he "went to the High Priest and applied for letters to the synagogues at Damascus authorizing him to arrest anyone he found, man or woman, who followed the new way, and bring them to Jerusalem" (Acts 9:1–2).

Legal righteousness is not unknown to any of us. Righteousness is the situation of being right with the law or standard or code or person or peer group that gives meaning to your life. Most of us pick something less than Paul's standard, which was the will of God as written in the law. Whatever you live by judges the worth of your life. The soldier who lives by his work has the obvious criterion of rank to tell him how well he is doing. Other professionals, doctors, lawyers, priests, have less overt, but equally telling, symbols that denote their success or failure: money, car, house, clothes, etc. The man who lives by the good opinion of peers depends upon professional or social standing to assure him that he is living the good life. If we live by our children, we must have them turn out well to feel right about ourselves. None of us have within ourselves the confidence that our existence is justified. We must gain justification by being right with some standard of authenticity. To fall short of the standard is to be guilty. The potential for self-righteousness is obvious: when guilt is the only game in town, your only hope of winning is to run hard enough to stay in front of the fellows behind you so you can make invidious comparisons between yourself and them.

—Paul, the Forgiven Sinner

Paul continued his self-portrait: "But all such assets I have written off because of Christ. I would say more: I count everything sheer loss . . . . I count it so much garbage, for the sake of gaining Christ and finding myself incorporate in him, with no righteousness of my own, no legal rectitude, but the righteousness which comes from faith in Christ, given by God in response to faith" (Phil. 3:7–9).

Righteousness by the book breaks down at the point I see marked against my name an F. The law, which gives us guidance to righteousness, also gives us consciousness of sin. At some point, Paul realized that "all men have sinned. For sin was already in the world before there was law, though in the absence of law no reckoning is kept of sin" (Rms. 5:12–13). The law, which defines sin, also condemns it and the sinner. Thus the law became the chain with which sin bound Paul, the noose that sin slipped around his neck.

"Except through law I should never have become acquainted with sin. For example, I should never have known what it was to covet, if the law had not said, 'Thou shalt not covet.' Through that commandment sin found its opportunity, and produced in me all kinds of wrong desires . . . . The commandment which should have led to life proved in my experience to lead to death, because sin found its opportunity in the commandment, seduced me, and through the commandment killed me" (Rms. 7:7–11). If the state of sin is one of alienation from God, the law actually increases sin by driving us into despair.

There may come a day when you, like Paul, experience yourself as unrighteous. There may come a day when you stand condemned, not even by God's standards, but by your own. It may be the day you do not get the long-anticipated promotion and perceive that you will never get it. It may be the day you realize that your marriage is failing. It may be the day you are rejected by that person or society or club you did everything you could to make yourself acceptable to. It may be the day your child so fails that you realize you have failed as a parent. It may be the day you commit an act you have always loathed others for committing. It may be the day toward the end of your life when you look back upon all that you have done, and the law you have lived by judges your entire life to have been a failure. The things you worked for did not happen. You never became the person you wanted to be. And you can offer nothing to justify yourself.

On that day you will experience a guilt and a humiliation that are immeasurable. If there is any act you can think of to atone for your failure, you will do it; but it will not be enough. If there were any way to make up for your failure, you would follow it; but there will be no way. And you will be tempted to embark upon a pattern of self-destruction in futile atonement, in vicious retribution, in unending expiation for the crime of failure.

On that day, remember what Paul discovered: the price of your failure has been paid. For our sake, Christ became a failure and has made our failure acceptable. He assumed the burden of our flesh that we might receive the freedom of his spirit. He has been rejected, publicly exposed, humiliated, whipped, scorned, spat upon and crucified in order that we need not do that to ourselves. On the day you find yourself unloved by anyone, including yourself, remember that you are infinitely loved by God who walked the way of the cross to find you. On the day when you are judged to be of no account, remember that you are precious to Christ who has purchased you with his very blood. The life you may no longer want to live, God will join to his own life and live through you. "What I mean is, that God was in Christ reconciling the world to himself, no longer holding men's misdeeds against them . . . . It is as if God were appealing to you through us: in Christ's name, we implore you, be reconciled to God! Christ was innocent of sin, and yet for our sake God made him one with the sinfulness of men, so that in him we might be made one with the goodness of God himself" (II Cor. 5:19–21).

Life in grace means that I surrender to God my standards and my laws, my virtues and my failures. It means I throw away my self-estimation and live from God's estimation of me. It means I surrender my pride and no longer seek justification from my children, my clubs, my clothes, my wealth, my beauty, my works, my competence, my wit, my friends, my strength, my righteousness. My life and worth are no longer grounded in anything that I do, in anything that I say, in anything that I feel, in anything that I earn or deserve, but solely in the blood of Jesus Christ that was shed for me. I live by faith from grace, sheer grace, nothing but grace.

—Paul, the Inspired Saint

Paul wrote to the church in Rome: "What the law could never do, because our lower nature robbed it of all potency, God has done: by sending his own Son in a form like that of our own sinful nature, and as a sacrifice for sin, he has passed judgement against sin in that very nature, so that the commandment of the law might find fulfillment in us, whose conduct, no longer under the control of our lower nature, is directed by the Spirit" (Rms. 8:3–4).

Once, an old, respected man, an educated and accomplished man named Nicodemus, came to see Jesus by night (he was also a cautious man) and was told, "Except a man be born again he cannot see the kingdom of God" (Jn. 3:3). He said similar things on other occasions. Once, "Jesus called a little child unto him and set him in the midst of them, and said, 'Verily I say unto you, except ye be converted and become as little children, ye shall not enter into the kingdom of heaven'" (Mt. 18:2–4; cf. Mk. 10:15, Lk. 18:17). Paul spoke of his own conversion as a rebirth. In recounting the appearance of the risen Christ to him, Paul said, "last of all as to one untimely born, he appeared even unto me who am the least of the apostles . . ." (I Cor. 15:8). Elsewhere, to the Galatians, Paul spoke of life in the Spirit as beginning with being "born after the Spirit" (Gal. 4:29).

To be born of the Spirit is to allow oneself to begin receiving from God the sort of life the law demanded but could not produce, and that we could not produce by our own best efforts. It is the beginning of a new life, a strange, wonderful, disorienting life. You spend your whole life learning how to control people, and then must begin all over again learning how not to be in control. What does the wind control (cf. Jn. 3:8)? You spend your whole life grabbing, and then begin all over again learning how to let go. You spend your whole life learning to assert yourself, then become born again and begin taking baby steps in accepting yourself. I spent my whole life acquiring tools and techniques of knowledge, but my spiritual pilgrimage has been one of living into the Mystery. We spend so much time learning how to achieve, then must begin again, like a little child, learning how to receive. We spend our whole lives learning how to guard and protect ourselves from each other and God; after rebirth we begin learning to be vulnerable. We spend our whole lives learning how to win, then must begin again learning how to surrender. We spend our whole lives acquiring the power to clobber our enemies only to have to start all over learning to love them. The bad news is that being born of the Spirit means starting all over; the good news is that, as Nicodemus heard, it is never too late. Moreover, the new life is eternal: "The harvest of the Spirit is love, joy, peace, patience, kindness, goodness, fidelity, gentleness and self-control . . . . If the Spirit is the source of our life, let the

Spirit also direct our course . . . . The man who sows seed in the field of his lower nature, will reap from it a harvest of corruption, but if he sows in the field of the Spirit, the Spirit will bring him a harvest of eternal life (Gal. 5:22–23, 25; 6:8; cf. I Cor.12:1, 31; 13:1–13).

Discipleship

To accept God's offer of eternal friendship and to embark upon the life of grace is what the church means by discipleship. Why do any of us hesitate? One reason is pride: we would rather do it on our own. Good luck. The other reason is fear. Someone once told me he had stood on the brink of discipleship for years, fearing that if he followed Christ, the Lord would strip him of his possessions, of which he had many. Finally he summoned up the courage to follow the Master anyway. "You know," he said, "Christ never took a thing from me. He just made all the things seem gradually less important. I have given away the boat I once feared losing; it became a burden."

In the end, of course, we lose it all anyway. We grow old. Our parents die, and then our friends. Our skin wrinkles and our muscles sag. Our bones grow brittle, and our joints ache. We retire from being a big man to become merely an old one. And then we die, leaving our possessions to others or the probate court. Our health, our wealth, our looks, our power, our wit, our charm—all these fall away in winter like leaves from a tree, leaving us stripped and bare. Happy in that day is the disciple who knows he goes from lesser to larger life. Happy in that day is the disciple who, though he lose the world, has gained his soul.

Happy in that day is the disciple who, having run with patience the race that was set before him, can go home to his Lord and be free.

THE BODY OF CHRIST

The phrase "body of Christ" refers to four things in the New Testament: (i) It can mean the physical body of the pre-resurrected Jesus of Nazareth (cf. Mk. 14:8, e.g.). This body is no different from the flesh-and-blood body of each of us. (ii) It could be used of Christ's resurrected body, which is not an ordinary flesh-and-blood body that we are familiar with. For one thing, it has the uncanny ability to appear suddenly in a locked room (Jn. 20:19, 26). For another thing, Christ, so embodied, is not at first recognized by his disciples (Lk. 24:14–16; Jn. 21:4–7). One might almost say that it is a body in the process of being transformed from flesh to spirit, from matter to energy. It is definitely a transitional stage between the pre-resurrected Jesus and the Christian Church. (iii) The Church herself is the third phase of Christ's body. (iv) The bread of the Lord's Supper is also the body of Christ[2] (cf. Lk. 22:19; I Cor. 11:24). It is a temple within the temple, so to speak, an incarnation within the ongoing incarnation, indeed the fuel for it. The differences among the four bodies are apparent: they are not the same body. Obviously, when I receive the eucharistic host I am not chewing the flesh of Jesus of Nazareth. What the four have in common, the reason they are all called "the body of Christ," is that they all embody Christ. Christ is just as really present in the consecrated bread of the eucharist as he was in the flesh and blood of Jesus of Nazareth. Christ is just as really present in his body the Church as he was walking with his disciples on the road to Emmaus.

> How vast [are] the resources of [God's] power open to us who trust in him. They are measured by his strength and the might which he exerted in Christ when he raised him from the dead, when he enthroned him at his right hand in the heavenly realms, far above all government and authority, all power and dominion, and any title of sovereignty that can be named, not only in this age but in the age to come. He put everything in subjection beneath his feet, and appointed him as supreme head to the Church, which is his body and as such holds within it the fullness of him who himself receives the entire fullness of God (Eph. 1:19–23).

The point of the doctrine of the ascension is not that the physical body of Jesus of Nazareth was taken into heaven (and where might that be?). The point is that Christ takes his humanity with him when he returns to the Father. The Incarnation was not a temporary phase in the life of God; the triune Godhead is permanently enriched with the addition of humanity. The Incarnation was what God had in mind all along. It continues on earth in the Church. The Incarnation begun in Jesus is intended to be not only a permanent but also an ever-growing reality, expanding to incorporate the whole human race. As the Holy Spirit engendered the Incarnation (Mt. 1:20; Lk. 1:35) and bound Jesus to the Father (Mk. 1:10–11), so he engenders the Church, animates the Church, unifies the Church and unites her to God. When the Church is co-extensive with the human race and the Incarnation has become all in all, there will be no God without man and no man without God. This is clearly what God has in mind. With this in mind, several corollaries follow.

Salvation Is Corporate, Not Individual

The Church as a whole is the successor to Christ, is the recipient of the Holy Spirit and the bearer of the Spirit. The Church is the charismatic. The Church is not a collection of individual believers. On the contrary, each of us becomes Christian by being incorporated into the Church, engrafted onto the Body of Christ. We miss the point of Pentecost if we think of a bunch of individuals sitting around talking in tongues. The Church as a whole is given the power and mission of preaching the gospel to all nations. There has been much nonsense, particularly in America, to the effect that once you give your life to Christ, you and he will form a complete whole. The Bible knows no such thing as a solitary Christian. No one person can fully embody the Holy Spirit. Any one person's experience of Christ is partial, his faith unfulfilled. "For Christ is like a single body with its many limbs and organs which together make up the body" (I Cor. 12:12). "There is one body and one Spirit as there is also one hope held out in God's call to you; one Lord, one faith, one baptism; one God and Father of all who is over all and through all and in all" (Eph. 4:4–6).

If Christianity is corporate, not individual, where does the individual fit in? "Now you are Christ's body, and each of you is a limb or organ of it" (I Cor. 12:27). The body of Christ is the corporate reality of the church; we truly participate in Christ only to the extent that we are part of his body, the Church. Each of us is only a limb or organ of the body. But, at the same time, each of us is crucial and irreplaceable in the body. The body cannot be whole without each one of us. "If the body were all eye, how could it hear? If the body were all ear, how could it smell?" (I Cor.12:17). For example, individuals represent different types of piety, all of which are necessary for the completeness of the body. Thinkers have a predominantly intellectual piety; their concern is to know God. They read a lot and take courses in the Bible and theology; they are always trying to better understand. Feelers, on the other hand, have a predominantly emotional piety and find God in the human heart. Their concern is to love God. They experience faith as being deeply moved. They pursue spirituality. They sing and weep and hug a lot. Then there are the doers, who have a moral type of piety. Their concern is to obey God. They express their faith in doing good works, feeding the hungry, protecting the environment, righting social wrongs. The body of Christ needs all these folk in order to be whole. Without intellectuals and moralists, the Church would be on a self-indulgent emotional jag without reference or relevance to truth or justice. Without the feelers and moralists, the Church would be just a philosophical society of dilettantes who endlessly speculate about God but have no impact on the world. Without the thinkers and feelers, the Church would be merely a grim and probably self-righteous effort to remake the world with little humor or warmth. The body needs all its members in order to be whole.

The Church Is the Community, Not the Building

We do not go to church; we are the Church. The Church is not a place; she is a who; she is us. No matter how long we have belonged to a church, so long as we think of the Church as a place or a they, we have not understood the Church and are not really part of her. So long as I merely go to worship to be entertained or inspired by the preacher and choir, I do not really belong to the Church. I become part of what Christ means by the Church when I have invested myself in the community sufficiently to have the opportunity to love the other members. At the Last Supper, Jesus said, "I give you a new commandment: love one another; as I have loved you, so you are to love one another. If there is this love among you, then all will know that you are my disciples" (Jn. 13:34f).

What does Jesus mean by love? Does he mean that we find one another attractive, that we fall in love with one another, that we send chills down each other's spines? Did the Good Samaritan fall in love with the man who was lying in the ditch (cf. Lk. 10:33ff)? What Christ means by love is being compassionate and helpful. St. Paul spoke often of love also; for it is what binds the Church together and to God. "Be generous to one another, tender-hearted, forgiving one another as God in Christ forgave you. In a word, as God's dear children, try to be like him, and live in love as Christ loved you, and gave himself up on your behalf as an offering and sacrifice . . ." (Eph. 4:32–5:1f). Forgiveness is particularly important. As Lord Herbert said, "He that cannot forgive others, breaks the bridge over which he, himself, must pass if he would ever reach heaven; for everyone has need to be forgiven."[3] Elsewhere St. Paul characterized love, the greatest gift of the Holy Spirit: "Love is patient; love is kind and envies no one. Love is never boastful, nor conceited, nor rude; never selfish, not quick to take offense. Love keeps no score of wrongs; does not gloat over other men's sins, but delights in the truth. There is nothing love cannot face; there is no limit to its faith, its hope, its endurance. Love will never come to an end . . . . In a word, there are three things that last forever: faith, hope and love; but the greatest of them all is love" (I Cor. 13:4–8, 13).

It Is Christ's Church, Not Ours

We are his body, but he is our head. A body whose limbs acted independently of the head would be spastic. Members of the Church should not ask of any policy or activity of the Church, "Does this please me?" but rather, "Will this please Christ?" The operative question for the Church is never, "What do we want to do this year?" but, "What does the Lord require of us? For what purpose does Christ employ his hands and feet?" We discover that through prayer and study. They are the nerves by which messages are transmitted from the head to the body. Without prayer and study, especially Bible study, Christ becomes quadriplegic. St. Paul concluded a list of ministries within the Church by saying that all were given to equip God's people for work in his service, to the building up of the body of Christ. So shall we all at last attain to the unity inherent in our faith . . .—to mature manhood, measured by nothing less than the full stature of Christ. We are no longer to be children, tossed by the waves and whirled about by every fresh gust of teaching . . . . No, let us speak the truth in love; so shall we fully grow up into Christ. He is the head, and on him the whole body depends. Bonded and knit together by every constituent joint, the whole frame grows through the due activity of each part, and builds itself up in love (Eph. 4:12–16).

THE HOLY CATHOLIC CHURCH

Her Hypocrisy

People sometimes tell me, "I don't go to church; it is full of hypocrites." I try to reassure them: "Not quite full; there is always room for one more." There is a fate worse than hypocrisy, and that is to reach for nothing beyond your grasp and to profess nothing nobler than you embody at the moment. The man who serves only himself has an increasingly unworthy master, eventually experienced as such. Those who dare to serve the King of Kings will always have hypocrisy as part of their vocation. Nevertheless it is disturbing to go to a church and find it full of people no better than yourself. Anyone who has been in the Church very deeply or very long has, on at least one occasion, listened to a stupid sermon, had his feelings hurt, been rejected, been slighted, been misunderstood, been turned off. A friend once told me, "I love the Church because she is my mother, but she is a whore." One palliative for the pain of realizing the Church's infidelity is to realize your own. When the sin is seen to be internal, one can begin doing something about it and, by doing so, improve the health of the whole body. The scandal of the Incarnation is not just that God becomes man but also that Christ chooses people like ourselves as his body. I myself never lost faith in the Church because I never had faith in her to begin with. I put my faith in God. The Church is not God. She is a sacrament; she points beyond herself. She must say with Paul, "It is not ourselves that we proclaim; we proclaim Christ Jesus as Lord and ourselves as your servants for Jesus' sake" (II Cor. 4:5).

Her Fidelity

After surviving some initial disgust at finding the Church to be more a hospital for sinners than a hotel for saints, I have been most surprised by the number of saints the Church does contain. One of the privileges of the priesthood is being able to get close enough to people to see the quiet nobility of many of them. Many Christians lay their lives down undramatically but daily, caring for a sick relative or for the sick who have no claim upon them. The Church's record over the centuries is not what Christ would want it to be. But compared to that of governments or other religions, it is not bad. Over the centuries the Church has founded schools, hospitals and orphanages, has ameliorated the conditions in prisons, insane asylums and the workplace, and has campaigned against cruelty. Is it a coincidence that modern medicine arose within Christendom? Is it a coincidence that restrictions were first placed on the untrammeled sway of government within Christendom, that documents like the Bill of Rights and the Universal Declaration of the Rights of Man were written in the West? Compare the number of charitable organizations and the number of volunteers who staff them in

Christian countries to those in the non-Christian world, and the Church's role looks not only good, but indispensable to the humaneness of our present world, such as it is.

God's Fidelity

Like all institutions, the Church grows corrupt in time. What is unique about the Church is that when she has grown so rotten that one swift kick would knock her over, she does not fall over. The kick knocks off the rot, revealing girders of steel beneath. The Holy Spirit blows in saints who renew Christ's body. When other institutions would collapse, the Church is reformed. The Christian Church is the oldest functioning institution in the world. She has seen the commencement of all the governments that now exist on the face of the earth. I have no doubt she shall live to see their end. The Church was vital, but already ancient, before Columbus made landfall upon this continent, before the Saxons had set foot in Britain, before the Franks had crossed the Rhine, and when Grecian eloquence still flourished in Antioch. No doubt she shall exist still in undiminished vigor when some tourist from New Guinea shall pause to photograph the ruins of Manhattan.[4]

The Movement into God

Christ points us to the Father.

WORSHIP

"Offer to God a sacrifice of thanksgiving, and make good your vows to the Most High" (Ps. 50:14). "Ascribe to the Lord the honor due his Name; bring offerings and come into his courts" (Ps. 96:8). "I appeal to you, brethren, by the mercies of God, to present yourselves as a living sacrifice, holy and acceptable to God, which is your spiritual worship" (Rms. 12:1). Our ancient fathers in the faith would be completely baffled by the modern notion of going to worship in order to be inspired or to get something out of it ("I went to church once, but I didn't get anything out of it"). To ancient Jews and Christians, worshipping God did not mean receiving something from him; it meant giving something to him. Worship is offering. Worship is acknowledging God's worthiness. In St. John the Divine's vision of the redeemed worshipping God in heaven, they are praising him: "O Lord our God, you are worthy to receive glory and honor and power; because you have created all things, and by your will they were created and have their being" (Rev. 4:11). So the first thing to get straight is the nature and proper motive for worship. A worship service is service to God not to us.

Secondly, corporate worship is the Church's worship in which we participate. We praise God in union with the Church all over the earth, the Church in all ages past and the Church in heaven. We praise him "joining with the heavenly chorus, with prophets, apostles and martyrs, and with all those in every generation who have looked to [God] in hope, to proclaim with them [his] glory in their unending hymn: Holy, holy, holy

Lord, God of power and might, heaven and earth are full of your glory."[5] Hymns are songs in praise of God. A song such as "I've got that joy, joy, joy, joy down in my heart, down in my heart" is not a hymn; it is a celebration of emotions.

Corporate worship is the body of Christ, in all times and places, praising the Father. But it is meant to be a full-body exercise in which all the members participate. I should never go to worship as a passive spectator to be entertained by the choir and preacher's performance. Insofar as worship is a performance, you and I are the performers and God is the audience. I make a mistake if I worship with the intention of getting something out of it, but that does not mean that I will not get anything out of it. God offers us his grace even as we offer him our praise.

THE SACRAMENTS
Embodiments of Grace

Christianity is not merely, or even primarily, a set of beliefs or a bundle of feelings or doing the right thing. Christianity is a relationship between God and man from which beliefs, feelings and actions proceed. God has the initiative in this relationship. We exist at all only at his creative initiative. We are reconciled to him only because he "stooped to save his lost creation and died on earth that all might live above."[6] The institutional Church exists only because Christ instituted her. Our role in the relationship is responsive and cooperative. Our initiative-taking God is incarnational; while being himself Spirit, he loves bodies. He loves human bodies so much that he made one for himself. "So the Word became flesh; he came to dwell among us, and we saw his glory, such glory as befits the Father's only Son, full of grace and truth" (Jn. 1:14). When Christ returned to the Father, he did not leave us comfortless; he left us the sacraments.

The physical is not anti-spiritual; it is the means of making spirit concrete. The sacraments are concrete, physical, visible, tangible, tasteable embodiments of God's grace, that is, of his life and love. They are little incarnations. They are the means whereby a spiritual God who loves bodies acts to possess and give himself to human beings who are body and spirit.

The sacraments are symbolic in that they point beyond themselves. There is more going on in baptism than just water being splashed on someone's head. God is acting through the water. But the outward and visible signs are important in themselves; water is a necessary part of baptism. We do not have just a spirit-to-spirit relationship with God. Neither the sacraments nor we are disembodied spirits. The sacraments embody the grace of the risen Christ.

The sacraments are not magic any more than Jesus was. One must believe in order to perceive. Even some who saw Christ heal a man blind since birth, remained blind to who Christ was (cf. Jn. 9). Faith is not a substitute for truth but a necessary means to it. The man who is spiritually blind may eat Christ's body and remain oblivious to Christ's presence, thus neither perceiving nor receiving him. The sacraments must be received in faith. But the sacraments are symbols, not illusions. There is a reality there to be perceived. The grace of Jesus Christ is present and available in the sacraments. The love of Christ is conveyed through them just as your lover's love is conveyed through a touch. The touch is not itself love, and may indeed exist without love. But the touch conveys the love. The sacraments are the way the risen Christ touches us, conveying his risen life to us.

At Christ's Command

Two of the sacraments are called "dominically instituted," because Christ not only invited us to do them, he told us to.

—Baptism

Jesus said: "Full authority in heaven and on earth has been committed to me. Go forth therefore and make all nations my disciples; baptize men everywhere in the name of the Father and the Son and the Holy Spirit, and teach them to observe all that I have commanded you" (Mt. 28:18f).

Baptism is a sacrament of belonging, and of birth. My youngest daughter was not just born; she was born into an identity, a relationship, a family. Before she even left the hospital, her identity tag read "Miranda Todd." She did not pick those names out; she was given her identity. She was a member of a family even before she knew what one was. Her mother and I had the initiative in our relationship with her. We brought her home from the hospital to a crib, a room, a place that had been prepared for her even before she was born. We held her, loved her, clothed her and fed her long before she was able to articulate to herself that she was being cared for. Not that she did not know she was loved; infants know. They respond to being held; they often respond by ceasing to cry. They respond to being fed; they grow.

Miranda could not live by bread alone, so she has had a second birth as well. We brought her to Christ in response to his invitation "Suffer the little children to come unto me and forbid them not; for of such is the kingdom of God" (Mk. 10:14). Dogs and cats do not need to be born again, because their physical birth is quite sufficient. They will naturally and instinctively grow up into full-blown dogs and cats. You do not see many cats who have fallen short of their full catness, who fail to be all that they were meant to be. But Miranda is a spiritual being as well as a physical one; so she needed to be quickened from above as well as from below (cf. Jn. 3:3). At her baptism she received a new identity. She was sealed by the Holy Spirit "and marked as Christ's own forever."[7] She can never be good enough to deserve it, and she can never be bad enough to undo it. She did nothing whatsoever to earn either her first birth or her second, her first identity or her additional one. But she did not have to. It was a matter of grace. She was only slightly more aware of her second birth than she was of her first one, but she really was born both times. Within Christ's family the Church, she is loved, cared for, fed. She responds to her nurturance: she is growing spiritually. Of course, I must still bring her on Sundays to be with her brothers and sisters in Christ. But she has gained access to her Father's table; why would I keep her from it?

—The Holy Eucharist

"For the tradition which I handed on to you came to me from the Lord himself: that the Lord Jesus, in the night of his arrest, took bread and, after giving thanks to God, broke it and said: 'This is my body, which is for you; do this as a memorial of me'" (I Cor. 11:23f).

So the Church continues, as she has done for well-nigh two thousand years, to break bread and share the cup as a memorial to the earthly Jesus and as an encounter with the risen Christ (cf. Lk. 24:30–31). In a continuous movement of sanctification, the Holy Spirit brings the heavenly banquet down to earthly altars and spreads it before us. We gather to feed upon him who told us:

> I am the bread of life. Your forefathers ate the manna in the desert and they are dead. I am speaking of the bread that comes down from heaven, which a man may eat and never die. I am that living bread which has come down from heaven; if anyone eats this bread he shall live for ever. Moreover, the bread which I will give is my own flesh; I give it for the life of the world . . . . Whoever eats my flesh and drinks my blood possesses eternal life, and I will raise him up on the last day. My flesh is real food; my blood is real drink. Whoever eats my flesh and drinks my blood dwells continually in me and I dwell in him (Jn. 6:48–51, 54–56).

At its deepest, the Christian life is a mutual indwelling between Christ and the Christian. The Holy Eucharist is the chief means and nurturance of this union.

Other Sacramental Rites

—Confirmation

Miranda will be my daughter for the rest of her life, whether she likes it or not. Her identity is indelible; there is nothing she can do about that. What she can do as she grows in freedom is to curse the day she was born into our family, and repudiate everything we are and stand for. She will have the same freedom in her relationship with God. She can love him or not. Obey him. Or not. She can sell her baptismal birthright for a mess of pottage. A place will always be reserved for her at Christ's table, but how much good will it do her if she never dines there? She cannot undo her identity as Christ's sister; she can use her freedom to renounce her role in that relationship.

I hope she will instead use her freedom to renounce "Satan and all the spiritual forces of wickedness that rebel against God, the evil powers of this world which corrupt and destroy the creatures of God, and all sinful desires that draw [her] from the love of God."[8] I hope she will choose to "turn to Jesus Christ and accept him as [her] Savior . . . , put [her] whole trust in his grace and love . . . , and promise to follow and obey him as [her] Lord".[9] If she does that, she will confirm her baptismal vows. God will then confirm her in the sense of strengthening her with the Holy Spirit to empower her for ministry. This mutual confirmation is what the sacrament consists of.

—Marriage

The phrase "unconditional love" is bandied about a great deal nowadays. But the only person we ever vow to love unconditionally is our spouse. Unconditional love means precisely to stick by someone "from this day forward, for better for worse, for richer for poorer, in sickness and in health, to love and to cherish, until we are parted by death."[10] Marriage involves a great sacrifice of childish desire; we renounce the opportunity of having many enticing relationships for the sake of getting to know one person down to his backbone. Thus, the spouse is the pearl of great price. Marriage brings us knowledge of one another's worst. If we use our knowledge to condemn, we quickly become one another's chief critic, judge and enemy. The Lord intends us to have mercy on our spouse's soul, to use our knowledge of his fear to encourage him, to use our knowledge of his guilt to forgive him. Though forgiveness is the crown of love, it is also the condition for any enduring love. It alone can heal the inevitable breaches of love that befall any married couple. It is forgiveness alone that encourages and enables my enemy to become my friend. To be loved most by the one who knows me best is grace indeed. Marriage is a sacrament, because it is a means of grace. My spouse stands as Christ to me, loving me as Christ has loved her (cf. Jn. 15:12). Thus it is wise for her to be rooted in Christ.

—Reconciliation

Judas betrayed our Lord once, and hanged himself (Mt. 27:5). I don't know what was wrong with Judas. I have betrayed Christ many more times than he did, but have been spared Judas' fate by using the sacrament of Reconciliation. No one must use this sacrament; all can; some should. The general confession we say at corporate worship is the Church confessing her sins in generalities: "We have not loved you with our whole heart; we have not loved our neighbors as ourselves. We are truly sorry and we humbly repent."[11] My individual sins are included in the generalization, but I may not experience forgiveness of them because I have kept them secret (though they are not secret from God; he watched me while I was doing them). The sacrament of Reconciliation is for me individually. I can name and receive absolution for specific sins ("I robbed a bank"; "I killed a man"; "I committed adultery"; "I perjured myself") that have bedeviled my conscience for years.

In beginning to repair to this sacrament, it is helpful to focus on the "biggies": actions that caused serious injury to someone else, that you knew were wrong at the time you did them, and that you were free not to do. Later, it is helpful to get behind the actions to the attitudes (avarice, anger, lust, etc.) that gave rise to them.

This is the sacrament of the Prodigal Son.[12] To use it is to get an accurate picture of where we are, to come to ourselves, and to get up and head for home. One need not have done anything horrible to receive the grace of reconciliation. Jesus did not say, "Repent because you are horrible people"; he said, "Repent; for the kingdom of God is at hand" (cf. Mk.1:15). In other words, something magnificent is being offered to us, but we may not be in a position to receive it.

I sometimes think of this sacrament as akin to doing the laundry. When my clothes and bedclothes get dirty, I do not go into hysterics. I do not wring my hands and weep and cry out "Oh, the sheets are dirty! My pants are dirty! The towels are dirty!" On the other hand, I do not get defensive and say, "There's nothing wrong with those sheets!" I just sort them out and take them to the laundry. The priest is the launderer. He is not there as your judge; he is there as a representative of Christ's mercy. Or, to shift the analogy, he is a garbageman. You dump your garbage in front of him, and he carts it off.

Three things are required of you in order to avail yourself of reconciliation. The first is contrition, which means that you wish to God you had not done what you did. The second is faith, a willingness to turn to Christ again and rely upon him (sins arise from misplaced love). The third thing is a willingness to have mercy on your fellow servant (Mt. 18:23ff), to forgive those who have sinned against you. Forgiveness of sins is the greatest power Christ asserted for himself and later committed to the Church (Jn. 20:23). We are all meant to be bearers of it. Many of us have been seriously injured by someone who is living in hell because of his sin. We have power to release a soul from hell. It is true that he cannot receive our forgiveness without contrition; it is also true that sometimes forgiveness precedes contrition. Jesus forgave a man who did not even know he was paralyzed by sin (Mk. 2:1–12).

—Unction

This sacrament, the laying-on of hands and anointing of the sick, brings Christ's healing touch to bear upon our internal disarray, psychological, physical and spiritual. It is intended for use in addition to, not in place of, whatever miracles of modern medicine may be helpful. Physical healing that comes is, of course, temporary; our bodies, like our baby teeth, have a built in obsolescence. The sacrament's greatest balm is the healing of our souls, which shall be new clad in the Resurrection (cf. I Cor. 15:35–37).

—Holy Orders

The Holy Spirit empowers various orders of ministry in the Church. The most important is that of lay people, who make up 99 percent of the Church. They are to convert the world and carry out Christ's ministry of reconciliation within it. Lay people receive ordination for their apostolate in the sacrament of Baptism. The other three orders of ministry in the Church exist for the sake of the lay ministry. Bishops represent Christ in guarding the faith, discipline and unity of the church, and they ordain others to their ministries. Priests represent Christ in the local parish, and administer the sacraments of baptism, eucharist, reconciliation and unction. Deacons represent Christ's ministry of servanthood.

All the sacraments are means whereby God's grace is brought to bear upon us and, through us, upon the world. They are vehicles of the Holy Spirit's love, giving integrity to the individual, unifying the Church, and bringing the world into unity with God.

SPIRITUALITY

The ground of all being became human being in Jesus of Nazareth, partly to provide focus for our devotion. But he could not remain among us in physical form forever, lest Jesus become an idol, lest he who came to be our way to the father become a dead end. So he, who came among us to provide increased intimacy with God, left in order to pave the way for the Holy Spirit, who increases our intimacy with God yet further. We know the risen Christ now through the Holy Spirit.

But before returning to the Father, Christ gathered his closest disciples around him to impress upon them what they most needed to remember. In his farewell discourse, Christ told them: "I am the vine and you are the branches. He who dwells in me as I dwell in him, bears much fruit" (Jn. 15:5). Christianity is not essentially a new law. If it were, it would not be good news because the new law of love is harder to keep than the old law of justice. Christianity is primarily a mutual indwelling between Christ and the Church, a feeding upon the life of the risen Christ, that we may incorporate him into ourselves and grow in his likeness.

Americans have a can-do attitude, so it is doubly important for us to listen carefully to our Lord's instructions: "He who dwells in me as I dwell in him bears much fruit; for apart from me you can do nothing." Christ does not hand us the ball and say, "Okay, now you run with it." He does not send us out to be good or to do the right thing, but rather to be transmitters of his life and to bear specifically those fruits of faith, hope and love which result from his life flowing through us as sap flows through the branches of a vine. It is necessary to be rooted in Christ. Before saying anything to us about our activity, Christ counsels us about our resting-place: "Dwell in me, as I dwell in you" (Jn. 15:4).

The inner life is crucial to a Christian. Christ makes his risen life available to his disciples through the sacraments, through study, through membership in the community, and through prayer, meditation and contemplation. Prayer is talking to God about whatever is on our minds and in our hearts. It does not have to sound pious or religious; honesty and candor will be more effective. On the other hand, it is also a good idea to pray in union with Christians in ages past. Use of prayers in a book such as The Book of Common Prayer enables us to have our thoughts and feelings shaped by the ancient Psalmist and by saints throughout history, and to pray with the mind of the Church. Meditation is mental prayer, in which we focus our minds on an aspect of God's personality, or one of Christ's sayings, and let it resonate in our souls. Contemplation "is not a matter of thinking much but of loving much."[13] In contemplative prayer, we do not speak to God or think about him; we sit still in his presence, and listen to him with loving hearts. It is prayer without words or images.

Our ministry will be made effective, finally, not by our good intentions, or by our energy, determination or intelligence, but by the grace of God in Jesus Christ through the Holy Spirit, which will flow through us if we will but rest in God. Matthew Fox, paraphrasing Meister Eckhart, wrote: "Why is it that some people do not bear fruit? It is because they are so busy clinging to their egotistical attachments and so afraid of letting go and letting be that they have no trust either in God or in themselves.

"Love cannot distrust. It can only wait the good trustfully. No person could ever trust God too much. Nothing people ever do is as appropriate as great trust in God. With such trust, God never fails to accomplish great things."[14]

The Movement into the World

Christ points us to the neighbor: "Dear friends, let us love one another, because love is from God. Everyone who loves is a child of God and knows God, but if a man says 'I love God', while hating his brother, he is a liar. If he does not love the brother whom he has seen, it cannot be that he loves God whom he has not seen. And indeed this command comes to us from Christ himself: that he who loves God must also love his brother" (I St. Jn. 4:7–9, 20–21).

EVANGELISM

"Go forth therefore and make all nations my disciples" (Mt. 28:19). The good news is not to be kept secret; if it had been, the world would be much different than it is, and we would never have heard of Christ. The world needs to be reconverted in every generation. The world needs Christ today more than it

ever has; for at 5:29 a.m. on July 16, 1945, in the desert near
Alamogordo, New Mexico, man detonated the first atomic
bomb. The temperature at the center of the explosion "was four
times that at the center of the sun and more than 10,000 times
that at the sun's surface . . . . The radioactivity emitted was equal
to one million times that of the world's total radium supply."[15]
Watching it, the physicist who headed up the project recalled
a fragment from the Bhagavid-Gita: "I am become Death, the
shatterer of worlds."[16] The explosion marked the moment when
human knowledge so outstripped human wisdom that mankind
was brought to the edge of a precipice, where we shall teeter
evermore until we plunge into the abyss or turn to him who says,
"I am the way; I am truth and I am life" (Jn. 14:6). Warheads
a thousand times more deadly than that dropped on Hiroshima
have been built; thousands of them are now stockpiled, nay,
aimed at us and by us. Peace is no longer a dreamy ideal; it is a
necessity. But there will be no peace among men until there is
peace within them. We will know peace when we have become
subjects of the Prince of Peace.

On an individual level, evangelism has been compared to
one beggar telling another where to find bread. It obviously
should not be a matter of laying a trip on someone. It is one
friend telling another of what has been of great help to him. It
requires sensitivity to the needs and receptivity of the friend.
And precisely because faith is so personal, it also involves risk
of painful misunderstanding and rejection. But why should
love be risk-free?

THE WORKS OF MERCY

Christian love is not solely, or even primarily, a feeling. It is a movement of the will that entails actions: "My children, love must not be a matter of words or talk; it must be genuine and show itself in action" (I St. Jn. 3:18). "My brothers, what use is it for a man to say he has faith when he does nothing to show it? Can that faith save him? Suppose a brother or a sister is in rags with not enough food for the day, and one of you says, 'Good luck to you, keep yourselves warm, and have plenty to eat', but does nothing to supply their bodily needs, what is the good of that? So with faith; if it does not lead to action, it is in itself a lifeless thing" (James 2:14–17).

"God loved the world so much that he gave his only Son, that everyone who has faith in him may not die but have eternal life" (Jn. 3:16). But God also created this mortal life and has provided the bountiful earth to sustain it. Christ not only preached good news to the poor, but he also fed them and healed them and commanded us to do likewise. It would be insane to pit against each other the twin aspects of the Church's external mission, namely, evangelism and outreach. Some people say that the Church's mission is to feed the hungry, and so reform society that the hungry can feed themselves. Others insist that, no, the Church's mission is to convert the world, soul by soul, to Jesus Christ. But nothing is clearer in the New Testament than that both these things are the Church's mission; either one without the other is a truncation of our calling.

Evil and suffering are not theoretical problems to God. They are practical problems to which he responds in person. We do God no favor by attributing the evil and suffering he abhors to some humanly imagined master plan of his. He does not want us to theologize about evil; he wants us to help him eliminate it. He does not ask us to explain suffering but to alleviate it. He especially does not want those who are rich to romanticize poverty to the poor. "For you know how generous our Lord Jesus Christ has been: he was rich, yet for your sake he became poor, so that through his poverty you might become rich" (II Cor. 8:9).

Churches have food pantries and clothes rooms because we know that part of our mission is to feed the hungry, clothe the naked, visit the sick and the imprisoned (cf. Mt. 25:31–46). In other words, we are to respond to misery with mercy—which does not mean feeling teary-eyed, but doing the works of mercy.

In some cases, mercy will not take obvious forms. Forgiveness is always good for my soul, but the person who has sinned against me may need punishment. Christian love has the other's welfare for its object. If the other person is characteristically irresponsible and has been taking advantage of people's kindness for a long time, tough love may decide that he needs to be held accountable and suffer the consequences of his actions. Pity the child who has never been punished. Punishment, however, should never be vindictive. If I feed a hungry man, I may be enabling his alcoholism, postponing the day when he hits bottom and seeks help from the disease that will otherwise kill him. I may feed another hungry man in place of doing something of more benefit to him. If I give a man a fish, I have fed him for a day; if I teach him how to fish, I have fed him for a lifetime. Charity must be my motive, the other's welfare my object; the means of charity will vary from case to case.

HEALING SOCIETY

Church and State

Jesus largely ignored the state. To Pilate's threat, "Surely you know that I have authority to release you and I have authority to crucify you," Jesus replied, "You would have no authority at all over me if it had not been granted you from above . . ." (Jn. 19:10–11). This was both a put-down of Pilate and an acknowledgment that political authority is of God.

Jesus also said, "My kingdom does not belong to this world" (Jn. 18:36). For three hundred years, this saying was helpful to the Church. She regulated her own affairs along New Testament guidelines and obeyed state authority in which she had no voice. But when the Emperor Constantine became Christian and Christianity soon thereafter became the official religion of the Roman Empire, the Church found herself, for the first time, responsible for the health of a state. Christians found themselves in political authority. They had to wield political power. Ideally, this power rests upon the consent of the governed but, failing that, upon the ability to deprive citizens of life, liberty and property. What was the Church to do? The historical record of the Church's attempt to make Christ's kingdom of this world, and transform the city of man into the city of God, is not inspiring. At its worst, maybe during the Spanish Inquisition, people were tortured into confessing heresies for which they were then burned at the stake. We need not regret that Church and state are separate in the United States of America.

On the other hand, it is not sufficient to say that the Church should stay out of politics. I usually hear this opinion from parishioners after they have read in the newspaper that a bishop has said something politically relevant. The Church is the community of all baptized Christians; the complaining parishioners are as much the Church as the offending bishop is. Are they to stay out of politics? Are Christians not to run for office? Not to vote? There is neither Christian nor civic virtue in allowing by default the least devout to determine the ends toward which political power is applied. Nor is there virtue in allowing the least redeemed part of ourselves to sit in the seat of political power. Are we to vote only our pocketbooks? Our fear? Our greed? Defense contractors lobby Congress for more billions to build bombs. The dairy industry lobbies government to spend our taxes to buy up enough milk to artificially inflate the price we must pay for milk; with the profits thus gained, it hires more lobbyists to do more of the same. Is it illegitimate for Christians to ask Congress to vote funds to inoculate children against disease?

Nor does an oft-quoted saying of our Lord have relevance to our present political situation, though it once did. In the late 1700's, some Americans were trying to start a revolution over taxes. Their battle cry was, "No taxation without representation." First-century Jews had the same complaint against Rome. If

Jesus had been on our shores, he would have asked to see the coins with which the taxes were paid. Upon being handed a British shilling, he would have asked, "Whose head is this and whose inscription?" (Cf. Mt. 22:20). Upon being told, "George III's," he would have said: "Render therefore unto George III what is George III's and render unto God what is God's" (cf. Mt. 22:21). In other words, "Don't start killing people over this; it is just money." But that was a long time ago. Present-day Americans, secure in their own independence and prosperity, can only deplore other people's revolutions. Throughout the nineteenth century, America was looked upon as the nation that had fired the revolutionary shot heard round the world. Wherever people rose to throw off the shackles of tyranny, they shouted phrases reminiscent of those in our Declaration of Independence. But "since 1917, America has reversed her role in the world. She has become the arch-conservative power instead of the arch-revolutionary one. Stranger still, she has made a present of her . . . discarded role to the country which was the arch-conservative power in the nineteenth century . . . . America has presented her historic role to Russia."[17]

Revolution is a vomiting of the body politic, an attempt to expel a poisonous presence. The Church cannot applaud revolution because it involves murder and often results in conditions more unjust than those against which it was directed. But the Church should always, loudly and constantly, demand justice, which is the proper business of law and which, prevailing, obviates the necessity of revolution.

Justice

Justice requires not only that the laws be equally enforced among the weak and powerful alike but also that the laws themselves aim at the general welfare and not merely be whips by which the powerful maintain their position. In his first inaugural address, Thomas Jefferson said that a wise government "shall not take from the mouth of labor the bread it has earned."[18] Abraham Lincoln later extended the idea to prohibit one group of people from exploiting another:

> [There are] two principles that have stood face to face from the beginning of time and will ever continue to struggle. The one is the common right of humanity and the other is the divine right of kings. It is the same principle, in whatever shape it develops itself. It is the same spirit which says, "You toil and work and earn bread, and I'll eat it." No matter in what shape it comes, whether from the mouth of a king who seeks to bestride the people of his own nation and live by the fruits of their labor, or from one race of men as an apology for enslaving another race, it is the same tyrannical principle.[19]

Justice is the opposite of oppression, which is the exploitation of the weak by the strong, of the poor by the rich. The Bible considers oppression a form of stealing. As idolatry is the most frequently denounced sin against God, oppression is the most frequently denounced sin against man in the Old Testament. Oppression occurs when I, who have much, demand much of you, who have little, and pay you little for it. Because the law of supply and demand is simply the interaction between greed and desperation, Americans have seen fit to ameliorate it by minimum wage laws. A major reason America has been spared the revolution endemic to Central and South America is that our laws have prevented 10 percent of our population from being social parasites who, doing no labor themselves, live like bloated mosquitoes off the labor of the other 90 percent, who reap little reward for their toil. The apostle James warned oppressive Christians: "You have piled up wealth in an age that is near its close. The wages you never paid to the men who mowed your fields are loud against you, and the outcry of the reapers has reached the ears of the Lord of Hosts. You have lived on earth in wanton luxury, fattening yourselves like cattle—and the day for slaughter has come" (James 5:3–5).

Mercy

Christ said that my greatness would not be determined by the number of my servants, but by the number of people I serve (cf. Mk. 9:35; 10:42ff). But it is crucial that my servitude be voluntary; otherwise I am enslaved. If I give my goods to the poor, I am being charitable; if the poor take my goods from me, I am being robbed. Christ forgave the repentant thief on the cross (Lk. 23:39–43), but he did not endorse robbery. If I choose not to press charges against the man who robs me, I am being forgiving; if the state fails to press charges against the man who robs me, I am being oppressed.

It is difficult to put mercy into law. The law should never be less than just. Mercy goes beyond justice. It is difficult for the law to go beyond justice without falling below it. A merciful society will not take unlimited vengeance upon those who break its laws; but society must enforce its laws, lest it leave the law-abiding at the mercy of the least merciful within society. A merciful society will not wish to see even the least deserving starve; but it is not merciful to encourage those who could feed themselves not to.

The law is coercive; love is not. There are no easy guidelines for enlisting law in the service of love. What is clear is that the powerful should protect the weak instead of exploiting them and, better yet, should empower the powerless in order that they need not be dependent upon the mercy of the powerful. God employed his great power to give us life. In Christ, he came to show those who would be god-like what being God in human form is like. And through the Holy Spirit, God shares his power with us.

VII. Hope

The End of the World

VII. HOPE
A. The End of the World
    1) THERE WILL BE AN END
    2) DO NOT ANTICIPATE THE END
    3) LIFT UP YOUR HEADS
B. Heaven and Hell
    1) WHAT HAPPENS TO US WHEN WE DIE?
    2) WHAT HAPPENS TO NON-CHRISTIANS?
    3) WHAT HAPPENS TO THE WICKED?
C. Summary: The Christian Vision of Life
D. A Song of Celebration

Hope is faith projected into the future. The Church's mission is to convert the world and, solely by the force of love, transform it into the kingdom of our Lord Jesus Christ. If the mission seems fantastic, it is worth remembering that the Church converted the Roman Empire without force of arms. Who, watching Pilate condemn Jesus, could have imagined that two thousand years later Pilate would be remembered only because of that act whereas buildings devoted to the adoration of Christ would grace every continent of the earth?

In some times of great distress, the Church has given up hope of converting the world and has instead looked forward to its end. Such a time occurred during the imperium of Domitian toward the end of the first century AD. The Church was under vicious persecution from this, the first of many panoplied potentates who thought to exterminate Christianity. Christians were invited either to abjure Christ and burn incense to Domition's image or die. In such circumstances St. John the Divine, sitting on the isle of Patmos, wrote the Book of Revelation. For all its numerology, fantastic imagery, and convoluted cycles within cycles, the essential message of the book is simple: "Do not lose hope. We are surrounded by Romans on every side; they outnumber us a thousand to one and a great battle is about to begin. When it is over, there sure are going to be a lot of dead Romans lying around. God will soon replace this sordid sphere with a new heaven and a new earth where Christ will reign supreme together with those who have kept faith with him." For all its despair of converting the world, St. John's message is one of hope for the Church. It is understandable that St. John could not envision that the city of Rome itself would one day be the capital, not of a political empire, but of the largest Church on earth. Revelation is a good book to read in times of persecution. Why it and similar apocalyptic writings are enjoying such vogue today is a question worth pondering.

Jesus himself did not speak much of the end of the world. His teaching on this subject is contained in but one chapter in each of the gospels of Matthew (Ch. 24), Mark (Ch. 13) and Luke (Ch. 21). Jesus says essentially three things about the end of the world.

THERE WILL BE AN END

Jesus' whole discourse was occasioned by the disciples' admiration of the Jerusalem temple. The disciples were all boys from the hill country newly arrived in the capital city. Before their wondering eyes stood the Jerusalem temple, one of the more impressive sights in the ancient world. Forty years in the making and not yet finished, some of its huge blocks of green and white marble measured 67 1/2 feet in length, 7 1/2 feet in height and 9 feet in width. The eastern front and part of the sidewalls were covered in gold plate, flashing in the sun. As the disciples oohed and aahed, Jesus said, "Yes, look at it all. I tell you this: not one stone will be left upon another; all will be thrown down"(Mt. 24:2).

The end will come. As Shakespeare later put it: "The cloud-capped towers, the gorgeous palaces, the solemn temples, the great globe itself, yea, all which it inherit, shall dissolve, and . . . leave not a rack behind."[1] Scientists tell us that stars have a life cycle and some day our sun will exhaust its nuclear fuel and balloon into a red giant twenty-five times its present size. Meanwhile the earth's surface water will boil; the oceans and air will evaporate into space as the earth's crust heats to a thousand degrees. All that will happen in God's good time four to six billion years in the future.[2]

Long before then of course we may have preempted the sun's exhaustion by thermonuclear catastrophe.

Some say the world will end in fire,
Some say in ice.
From what I've tasted of desire
I hold with those who favor fire.
But if it had to perish twice,
I think I know enough of hate
To say that for destruction ice
Is also great
And would suffice.[3]

Whether through the obsolescence of the sun or the fire of human passion or the ice of human hate, the end will come.

DO NOT ANTICIPATE THE END

Jesus tells us not to speculate about the end of the world. For one thing, such speculation is futile. "But about that day or that hour no one knows, not even the angels in heaven, not even the Son; only the Father" (Mk. 13:32). Those who make their living correlating the Near East's penchant for turning its cities into rubble with obscure references in the Book of Revelation are wasting their time. But since the writers turn a profit from their readers' gullibility, perhaps it would be more accurate to say that those who read such efforts are wasting their time.

Do not speculate about the end. Such speculation is not only futile, it is also unnecessary. The Son of Man will not be hiding in the wilderness. "Like lightening from the east, flashing as far as the west, will be the coming of the Son of Man . . . . The sun will be darkened, the moon will not give her light, the stars will fall from the sky . . ." (Mt. 24:27, 29). In other words, you will know when it is happening.

Do not anticipate the end. It is futile; it is unnecessary; and the destruction of the world is nothing to look forward to with joy. It will be a terrifying, horrible experience, "men's hearts failing them for fear" (Lk. 21:26). "Alas for women with child in those days, and for those who have children at the breast! Pray that it may not be in winter when you have to make your escape, or Sabbath. It will be a time of great distress; there has never been such a time from the beginning of the world until now . . ." (Mt. 24:19–21). The people who scare me to death are those who eagerly await the end of the world and have already decided that a thermonuclear war would be the long-prophesied Battle of Armageddon. I fear there are some who would gladly push the button as a pious act to help things along and to rescue themselves from the ambiguity of living in the twenty-first century. I feel sure the Lord will account us bad stewards indeed if we hand his creation back to him as a pile of radioactive ashes. The world is to be cared for by us, not destroyed. Life is to be lived to its fullest, not backed off from or weaseled out of or ended prematurely. Do not anticipate the end.

LIFT UP YOUR HEADS

Jesus' final message is this: when the end does come, if the worst should happen, if you should one day be blinded by the rockets' red glare, the bombs bursting in air, "then look up and lift up your heads; for your redemption draweth nigh" (Lk. 21:28 KJV). The world will end for each of us before it ends for all of us. When the end does come, when the lump proves to be malignant, when the floor beneath your feet, yea the earth itself, begins to quake—dishes flying off the shelves and the roof caving in upon you—"then look up, and lift up your heads; for your redemption draweth nigh." The same Lord who leads us beside the still waters comes to meet us as well walking across the turbulent sea when the boat is about to sink.[4] The God who is present in the gentle breeze is present as well in the tornado. One Christian's violent death and another's quiet demise are alike entrances to God's eternal kingdom. The Christian soul, incarnate as it is in frail flesh and blood, must seem a fleeting thing in comparison to the solid earth. But the almighty God who has made them both has fashioned the earth for dissolution and the soul for eternal life.

In the meantime, the time of this mortal life, let us "seek him who made the Pleiades and Orion, and turns deep darkness into the morning, and darkens the day into night; who calls for the waters of the sea and pours them out upon the surface of the earth: The Lord is his name" (Amos 5:8). Someone said that though we cannot know what the future holds, we can know him who holds the future. We cannot know the end of the world; we can, even now, turn to him who is our end.

> At the round earths imagin'd corners, blow
> Your trumpets, Angells, and arise, arise
> From death, you numberless infinities
> Of soules, and to your scattered bodies goe,
> All whom the flood did, and fire shall o'erthrow,
> All whom warre, dearth, age, agues, tyrannies,
> Despaire, law, chance, hath slaine, and you whose eyes,
> Shall behold God, and never taste deathes woe.
> But let them sleepe, Lord, and mee mourne a space,
> For, if above all these, my sinnes abound,
> 'Tis late to ask abundance of thy grace,
> When wee are there; here on this lowly ground,
> Teach mee how to repent; for that's as good
> As if thou hadst seal'd my pardon, with thy blood.[5]

Meditating upon the end of my life can lead me to the beginning of life.

Heaven and Hell

Ancient science thought the universe was three-tiered. The earth was a flat disk floating on the waters under the earth. Above the earth, supported by four pillars, was a solid dome (firmament) punctured with holes to let through some of the waters above the firmament (rain). The dome was also spangled with stars, which together with the sun and the moon, made their way across the firmament at different times and at different rates of speed.

God lived up there in heaven. Some Greeks thought the gods lived on top of Mt. Olympus, the highest mountain in Greece. All high mountains were close to the heavens. So mountaintops were likely places for religious experiences and many of them became holy places (Mt. Sinai, Mt. Tabor, Mt. Gerizim, Mt. Zion). The Hebrews may not have been too sophisticated scientifically, but they knew God well enough to know his heavenly dwelling was beyond the creation not within it. Early on, the Hebrews had a firm grasp of God's transcendence. So to them heaven was higher than just the sky, let alone a mountaintop. Today we know that beyond the sky, in all directions from the earth, blank space stretches for millions of light years beyond the horizon of human ken. Where then is heaven?

Heaven is today, as it always has been, where God is. But where is God? Everywhere. Up there, down here, around us and within us. "O holy God behind the silent stone, Beneath the under and the elder fire, Beyond the Milky Way, within the bone, The grace desired and grace of our desire."[6] Location is not an attribute of God. Location means to occupy space. Nothing can be located in two places at the same time, and no two things can occupy the same space. Neither of these statements is true of God. He always is everywhere and "in him we live and move, in him we exist" (Acts 17:27). Since God is not located, heaven is not a place. To be in heaven is to be where God is, to be with him, to be close to him, to be united to him in love.

Some ancient people thought that departed spirits went to a subterranean location. The Greeks called it "Hades"; and the Hebrews, "Sheol." Volcanos and geysers gave hint that Hades might be hot. Since God was up there in heaven, those who were down in Sheol were far from him. But even some ancient Hebrews began to see that this model was too simplistic. Speaking from his own religious experience, the Psalmist prayed:

Whither shall I go then from thy spirit?
Or whither shall I flee from thy presence?
If I ascend up into heaven, thou art there;
If I make my bed in hell, behold, thou art there.
If I take the wings of the morning
and dwell in the uttermost parts of the sea,
Even there shall thy hand lead me,
and thy right hand shall hold me (Ps. 139:7–8 KJV).

Where is hell? It is being far from God, being alienated from him, cut off from the source of life, deprived of what is most dear. To the man who has set his heart on his power, possessions and prestige, death itself would be a great deprivation; "for, we brought nothing into this world, and it is certain we can carry nothing out" (I Tim. 6:7 KJV).

The question of heaven and hell is really the question of our eternal destiny.

WHAT HAPPENS TO US WHEN WE DIE?

We cannot know for sure what happens to us when we die since death is "the undiscover'd country, from whose bourn no traveller returns"—none save one.[7] But some people have returned from the borders of death. Books like *Life after Life* contain the testimonies of people pronounced clinically dead and then revived.[8] The people brought back to life tell of having left their bodies and looking down upon them from above. Then they are met by others embodied not in flesh and blood but in a sheath of light or in "light-filled bodies." It is interesting that light or luminescence is what the word *glory* primarily means in the Bible. God's glory is often described as a visible radiance. When Moses had seen the glory of God, his face shone (Ex. 34:29, cf. Ex.16:10; 33:18, 22; 40:34); when the shepherds abiding in the fields heard from God, "the glory of the Lord shone round about them" (Lk. 2:9 KJV).

Jesus did not return to this life from the borders of death. He went all the way in, down to the depths of Sheol, so to speak. And he did not return to this mortal life but appeared to his disciples from a life beyond this one and beyond death. He continues to "appear" through the Power of Life, the Holy Spirit. Christ's resurrection means that it is possible for a human life to be so infused with the divine life that it is transformed into eternal life. The resurrection means that we may have a power source available to us more potent than modern medicine or self-actualization seminars. The resurrection means that the very last event in your life may not be the one where you are lying in the hospital with all the tubes stuck in you with the respirator going in and out. I do not mean to belittle the dignity of death, which may be as uncomfortable and traumatic as the other miracle[9] when the waters that had protected you from the shocks of life suddenly ran out and you found yourself squeezed and pushed where you did not want to go. You were rudely shoved into what we call light; but you were blinded by it. You lay squalling in what we think of as normal temperature but at the time seemed very cold to you. Do you remember all that? No? Well, you will probably not remember your dying either; you will have better things to do. The first miracle we called your birth, and we all celebrated it. The second miracle we will call your death, and we will all cry because we will still be in the womb and will not know where you have gone and we will miss you. I do not want to belittle the dignity of death, but neither do I want to accord it more dignity than it deserves. Christ dealt a blow to death's dignity from which it is still trying to recover. Death, the intimidator of God's people and stock in trade of all tyrants, has not seemed quite so formidable since Christ trampled it underfoot on Easter morning. It just may not be the last word.

But, you may ask, how are the dead raised? In what kind of body? How foolish! The seed you sow . . . is not the body that shall be, but a naked grain, perhaps of wheat, or of some other kind; and God clothes it with the body of his choice, each seed with its own particular body . . . . There are heavenly bodies and earthly bodies; and the splendour of the heavenly bodies is one thing, the splendour of the earthly, another . . . . So it is with the resurrection of the dead. What is sown in the earth as a perishable thing is raised imperishable. Sown in humiliation, it is raised in glory; sown in weakness, it is raised in power; sown as an animal body, it is raised as a spiritual body . . . . This perishable being must be clothed with the imperishable, and what is mortal must be clothed with immortality. And when our mortality has been clothed with immortality, then the saying of Scripture will come true: "Death is swallowed up; victory is won!" "O Death, where is your victory? O Death, where is your sting?" . . . God be praised, he gives us the victory through our Lord Jesus Christ (I Cor. 15:35–38, 40, 42–44, 53–55, 57).

Is such a thing possible? Can spirit survive flesh? Can energy exist without matter? Of course. Energy preceded matter; matter is just a form of energy. God is and he has no flesh. Can God reclothe our spirits in glorified bodies? Since he clothed them in flesh to begin with, it seems unlikely that he cannot reclothe them in form closer to his own. Is the God who created being out of nothingness and led his people through the wilderness impotent to lead them through the valley of the shadow of death as well?

But will he? I cannot believe that the God who called his people to himself with such patience over so many centuries would be content to commit us finally into any hands but his own. Did he walk the way of the cross to reclaim us for himself only for the brief span of this mortal life? We may say at least this much: both history and reason give us cause for confidence that when we have spun our last thread on earth, we fly not to nothingness but into the arms of our Father.

WHAT HAPPENS TO NON-CHRISTIANS?

Christianity inherited Judaism's intolerance, which is why Christians joined Jews in refusing to worship the Roman Emperor even alongside God. "You shall have no other god to set against me" (Ex. 20:3), the first commandment said. But whereas Jews soon kept to themselves, Christians set out to convert the world. Over the centuries missionaries were sent to every nation on earth because the Church believed Jesus' words as reported in The Gospel of John: "I am the way; I am the truth; and I am life; no one comes to the Father except by me" (Jn. 14:6). Recently some Christians have called this "religious imperialism" into question, especially since it has been often contaminated by cultural and political imperialism. Since World War I, the most sanguinary war in world history to that point, was begun and fought largely among nominally Christian countries, other nations have asked us to stop posing as the bearers of light. And some sophisticated Christians have asked us to respect other religions as valid ways to the Father.

An intolerance that automatically assigned all non-Christians to hell has in some quarters been replaced by universal tolerance, which teaches that the important thing is to be sincere in your faith no matter what it is. But do all roads lead to heaven?

If I want to get from Houston to Los Angeles and drive north on IH 45 in the sincere but mistaken belief that that is the way to get there, where will I wind up? Dallas perhaps; Oklahoma City perhaps; Kansas City perhaps; but not Los Angeles. Will I fail to get to Los Angeles because somebody is being mean to me? No. I will not get to Los Angeles because only a few roads go there and IH 45 is not one of them. One of the more important questions in life is "Where are you trying to arrive at and will the path you are travelling get you there?" Do all study habits lead to graduation? Do all life styles lead to health? Do all value systems lead to fulfillment? Does all behavior lead to happiness? Sincerity is not a saving grace.

Neither is adherence to religion, as such. I was naive enough to rejoice when the Ayatollah Khomeini took over Iran. I thought, "How nice that a religious man has replaced a dictator." Now when someone tells me he has given his life to God, I feel like barricading myself in my office until I find out what god he has given his life to and what that god requires of him. The ancient Aztecs were more religious than we are because they were willing to sacrifice their children to their gods whereas we will sacrifice ours only to national security or to obscure goals of foreign policy. But is child sacrifice the way to the Father? I do not think so. I hope not.

But what about the righteous pagan? Socrates? Siddhartha Gautama? The merciful non-Christian of your acquaintance? Jesus is reported to have said, "No one comes to the Father except by me." But what did he mean? John presents Jesus to us as perhaps he would have spoken were he aware of himself as the incarnate Logos. The Johannine Christ is the risen Lord known in the early Church. But we must turn to Matthew, Mark and Luke for the words of the historical Jesus and thus the interpretation of the Johannine saying. What did Jesus mean by "no one comes to the Father but by me?" Did he mean that we call ourselves Christian and stand up and publicly confess Jesus Christ as our Lord and Savior at a service of Confirmation or a revival? Did he mean that we call Jesus "Lord" to our family and co-workers at the office? Clearly not, because he plainly said, "Not everyone who calls me 'Lord, Lord' will enter the kingdom of heaven, but only those who do the will of my heavenly Father" (Mt. 7:21). We cannot just say something; we have to do something.

What does Jesus mean by "by me"? Does he mean get baptized? No, that is not enough either. Adolf Hitler was baptized. What went wrong? Was there not enough magic in that sacrament? There was never any magic in that sacrament. Baptism brought him into the Church, and it set little Adolf's feet on the path of Christ. But he strayed far from that path and wandered in a land that was waste and created a wasteland for millions. Christ represents a particular way of behavior; we must walk in that way. Christ embodies a particular truth about God and man; we must learn and embrace that truth. The risen

Christ offers us the very life of God; we must live that life. "I am the way; I am the truth and I am life; no one comes to the Father except by me" (Jn.14:6).

What is the way that is Christ? It is a way of faith in God. This faith, Jesus explains, means to trust God as a small child will trust and delight in his loving father. The way that is Christ is a way of compassion upon our neighbor who, as Jesus tells us in the parable of the Good Samaritan (Lk. 10:25–37), is anyone who needs us. The parable was occasioned by the very question we are addressing, "Master, what must I do to inherit eternal life?" (Lk. 10:25). The answer in short is "Love God and love your neighbor and you will live" (cf. Lk.10:27–28).

The question then becomes, can someone walk along the way that is Christ without knowing it is Christ's way? Can someone walk the way that is Christ without considering himself a Christian? Can one do so even while rejecting the invitation to call himself Christian? Can one do the will of the Father even while verbally rejecting the Father? Jesus says yes:

> But what do you think about this? A man had two sons. He went to the first and said, "My boy, go and work today in the vineyard." "I will, sir," the boy replied; but he never went. The father came to the second and said the same. "I will not," he replied, but afterwards he changed his mind and went. Which of these two did as his father wished? "The second," they said. Then Jesus answered, "I tell you this: tax-gatherers and prostitutes are entering the Kingdom of Heaven ahead of you" (Mt. 21:28–31).

Can Christ lead people who never heard of him to the Father? Yes. The faith of the Church and of the New Testament is that the Word who became Incarnate in Jesus of Nazareth existed long before the Incarnation. Indeed, "when all things began, the Word already was. The Word dwelt with God, and what God was the Word was. The Word, then, was with God at the beginning, and through him all things came to be; no single thing was created without him. All that came to be was alive with his life, and that life was the light of men" (Jn. 1:1–4). Christ is the agent of revelation whenever and wherever it occurs. There is but one God; so whoever worships God at all is worshipping the Father. Some folk, like the Aztecs, may have horribly distorted notions of God; indeed, we had no true image until the Incarnation. But insofar as people have a glimmering of God at all, it is vouchsafed them through Christ and the Holy Spirit.

Can people love Christ and serve Christ without knowing they are doing so? Can those who never saw Christ and never heard of him still receive the Father's blessing and enter the Kingdom? Jesus says yes:

> When the Son of Man comes in his glory and all the angels with him, he will sit in state on his throne, with all the nations gathered before him . . . . Then the king will say to those on his right hand, "You have my Father's blessing; come, enter and possess the kingdom that has been ready for you since the world was made. For when I was hungry, you gave me food; when thirsty, you gave me drink . . . ." Then the righteous will reply, "Lord when

was it that we saw you hungry and fed you, or thirsty and
gave you drink . . . ?" And the king will answer, "I tell you
this: anything you did for one of these my brothers here,
however humble, you did for me" (Mt. 25:31–40).

One of the very appealing qualities of these particular
righteous people is that they do not know they are righteous.
They are also amazed to discover that they have been loving
Christ all along. God, who can make children for Abraham
out of the very stones (cf. Mt. 3:9), welcomes the righteous
pagan.

Is righteousness then by works not faith? We must
remember that it was Paul, not Christ, who was so down on
works. But eternal life is not really a matter of reward for good
works performed. It is a matter of having gotten onto the up
escalator, by whatever means, instead of the down one.

Recall that man is the creature poised between divinity
and brutality. The good man is the virtuous one, the manly
man. The good human being is the humane one. He becomes
humane and fully human by living into the image of God in
which he was created (cf. Chapter IV:B). The Holy Spirit
enables us to do that; that is grace. But it is a matter of living
in the Spirit, not of calling it by the right name. Christ conveys
me to the Father and conveys to me the Father's love and life.
That is grace. Would Buddha have done the same? I do not
know, but having found a way to the Father, why would I want
to leave it to try another way? As Peter said, "Lord to whom
shall we go? You have the words of eternal life and we have

believed and come to know that you are the Holy One of God"
(Jn. 6:67 RSV).

Salvation is through faith, yes. But faith is discipleship not
magic. Faith is not a magic formula that one can recite whether
it be "abracadabra" or "I believe in God the Father Almighty,
maker of heaven and earth." Faith is not a magical ritual
one can perform whether it be the ablutions of the Pharisees
(cf. Mk. 7:1–8) or baptism. Discipleship does not mean just
wearing a little cross around our necks; it means picking up
our cross and following the way that is Christ to the Father.
Faith is discipleship by whatever name; discipleship is the up
escalator sharing the divine life.

WHAT HAPPENS TO THE WICKED?

The down escalator is brutality; it goes back to the
nothingness from which we have come. In the valley of Gihon
outside Jerusalem was the city garbage dump where trash
was always being burned and worms were in abundance. This
is the place Jesus seems to have had in mind in telling his
disciples: "If your hand is your undoing, cut it off; it is better
for you to enter into life maimed than to keep both hands and
go to hell (Gehenna) and the unquenchable fire" (Mk. 9:43,
cf. Mt. 18:8–9). Jesus was a story teller, not a systematic
theologian; he spoke in arresting images, not doctrines. The
doctrine of hell as a place of eternal torment was a product of
the medieval imagination. Jesus was talking about priorities
and was warning his disciples not to wind up on the garbage
dump. He meant what he said seriously but not literally. John

the Baptist used a similar vivid metaphor. He said that the Messiah will separate men as a reaper separates wheat from chaff. The wheat he will gather into his barn; the chaff he will burn (cf. Mt. 3:12; Lk. 3:17). When chaff is burned, it is reduced to nothing; it is not tortured for eternity. This mortal life itself is an unearned gift. God gives us the opportunity and graciously extends to us the means of arcing the gap between this mortal life and his own eternal life. "He has set fire and water before you; put out your hand to whichever you prefer. Man has life and death before him, which a man likes better will be given him" (Ecclus. 15:16f JB).

It seems most likely to me that the brutal just die and return to nothingness. Like a candle flame when extinguished, they do not go anywhere; they just go out. The other possibility is that the divine spark within all of us cannot gutter and all men have eternal life. What happens to the wicked then? To paint a picture of the unimaginable and speak spatially of what has no location, I would guess that in eternity those closest to God will be those most like him, the most compassionate. The most wicked will be farthermost from him. Their fate will be eternal congress with one another. Hitler, Stalin, Pol Pot, Idi Amin, Saddam Hussein, and Slobodan Milosevic can argue with ancients like Ozymandias about who is the greatest among them (cf. Mt. 20:25–28; Lk. 9:46–48). Pol Pot's feats of arms consisted solely of winning war against his own civilian population; so, I do not know how much glory the others will grant him. But come to that, most of Hitler's victims were civilians also. The victory he most prized was his murder of the defenseless Jews, Jesus' people, God's chosen. Elie Wiesel at age fifteen was taken to Auschwitz and has written his testimony in *Night*. When he arrived, another prisoner told him, "Poor devils, you're going to the crematory."

> He seemed to be telling the truth. Not far from us, flames were leaping up from a ditch, gigantic flames. They were burning something. A lorry drew up at the pit and delivered its load—little children. Babies! Yes, I saw it—saw it with my own eyes . . . those children in the flames . . . . I pinched my face. Was I still alive? Was I awake? I could not believe it. How could it be possible for them to burn people, children, and for the world to keep silent? . . . Never shall I forget that night, the first night in camp, which has turned my life into one long night, seven times cursed and seven times sealed . . . . Never shall I forget those flames which consumed my faith forever.[10]

Jesus' warning to his disciples was the end of an incident that began:

> At that time the disciples came to Jesus and asked, "Who is the greatest in the kingdom of Heaven?" He called a child, set him in front of them, and said, "I tell you this: unless you turn round and become like children, you will never enter the kingdom of Heaven. Let a man humble himself till he is like this child, and he will be the greatest in the kingdom of Heaven. Whoever receives one such child in my name receives me. But if a man is a cause of stumbling to one of these little ones who have faith in me, it were better for him to have a millstone hung round his neck and be drowned in the depths of the sea . . . . If

your hand or your foot is your undoing, cut it off and fling it away; it is better for you to enter life maimed or lame, than to keep two hands or two feet and be thrown into the eternal fire . . . . Never despise one of these little ones; I tell you, they have their guardian angels in heaven, who look continually on the face of my heavenly Father" (Mt. 18:1–6,8,10, cf. Mk. 9:42–48).

The people who caused the child Elie Wiesel to lose faith in God have much to answer for. The people who burned the children have much to answer for. In eternity, they will have no one to hate save those as hateful as themselves. Each will be surrounded and outnumbered by others as venomous as himself.

Can Hitler be redeemed? Sure, why not? God extends his mercy to all. Hitler will move incrementally toward God as he becomes incrementally more like him. To become like God is to become compassionate. Compassion is the willingness and ability to feel with your neighbor, to suffer his suffering. Hitler's journey into sanctity will consist of his experiencing the agony of each person the Nazis tortured to death, one by one. It will mean he dies the death, one by one, of each of six million Jews he murdered. It will mean his feeling with all his victims in all the countries the cold, the starvation, the pain, the terror he occasioned. As he increases in sanctity, he will be increasingly horrified and aghast at his sins, as the saints are at theirs. He will feel compelled to beg forgiveness from Elie Wiesel and from each soul he has harmed, one by one. It may take awhile.

Summary: The Christian Vision of Life

What ultimately happens to people of various sorts I do not really know. I do not have to know. It is not something I have to decide; in fact it is not something I get to decide. I am not God. The value of thinking about last things is to put present things in context. Without an end in mind, the present has no direction. Without direction there is no purpose; without purpose there is no meaning.

Someone has said, "without vision the people die." Do we have a vision of life today? Do images of the good life proffered us on television commercials constitute a vision? Over a century ago some intellectuals began to say that God was bad for the ego, his requirements burdensome, his presence oppressive. So our culture has gradually removed God from our worldview. Where there is no sense of what we ought to be, however, there is soon no sense of dignity about what we are. Life without requirements is meaningless and is soon experienced as such. Thus the Church has not been surprised to observe that, whereas medieval man experienced the human problem in terms of guilt, modern man experiences it in terms of meaninglessness. When man ceases to perceive the glory of God, he soon ceases to see the glory of man. Man apart from God soon becomes an object of contempt in his own eyes. Is it any wonder that modern fiction depicts man in restless, futile, constant quest, not for God, no longer believed in, but for a myriad of things that cannot be had apart from God: man in search of meaning, man in search of love, man in search of peace, man in search of himself? This last is particularly pathetic since, having removed his divine context, man has no points of reference by which to locate himself, let alone understand himself, let alone become himself. Detached from his divine depths, man accepts as profound what is shallow, as of great moment what is trivial and as silver, tinsel. And so nonfiction books about people are often no longer genuine biographies or autobiographies but the ghostwritten, confessional emesis of celebrities, people famous for being famous. It is as if, having disbelieved in God, man proceeded to debunk all his heroes and has been reduced at last to debunking himself. What picture of man is now thrown upon the silver screen? Is man in our movies noble? Is he honorable? Is he glorious? Is he a thing of beauty? Does he elicit our admiration and respect? Or does he at best, when pictured most sensitively and realistically, evoke only our pity (cf. *Death of a Salesman*)? Surely it is significant that the most admirable figures in contemporary cinema are plainly products of science fiction. Our creative geniuses stretch their faculties and come up with: Superman, a cartoon character. Is it any wonder that among growth industries are books and programs that promise to upgrade our self-image? But images of man are grotesque save for the image of God in which he was created, which Christ exemplified, which the Holy Spirit will help us actualize.

For a genuine alternative to the Christian vision of life, we must look past the present century to the tragic vision so eloquently enunciated by Shakespeare. Christianity is of course aware of the tragic dimension in life. A faith that springs from the graveyard, that focuses upon a young man unjustly crucified and that takes as its symbol the instrument of his torture can hardly be naive sentimentality—neither the sweet version (if you are a good girl, life will be good to you) nor the macho version (if you want it bad enough and are willing to pay the price, victory will be yours). Biblical people lived much closer to mortality and suffering than we do. Public executions were a common occurrence. Sights of lepers with digits and limbs fallen off were commonplace. Many children did not live to adulthood, and many mothers died in childbirth. Biblical people had all the diseases we do and some we no longer have. And they suffered them without benefit of antibiotics or any anodynes. The nearest thing they had to social security or insurance of any kind was the number, prosperity and charity of their children. Call them primitive if you will, but do not imagine for one moment that they were naive. So Christianity is well aware of life's ills listed by Hamlet:

> the slings and arrows of outrageous fortune . . .
> the whips and scorns of time,
> Th' oppressor's wrong, the proud man's contumely,
> The pangs of despis'd love, the law's delay,
> The insolence of office, and the spurns
> That patient merit of th' unworthy takes . . . . [11]

But, for all of that, the Christian does not view life as a tragedy. Macbeth said that life "is a tale told by an idiot, full of sound and fury, signifying nothing."[12] (cf. Chapter II:A1)

The Christian disagrees with this assessment. We believe that human life is a tale told ultimately by God himself. We are here today not because of a cosmic accident but because of a divine plan. There is a divine definition of humanity and a divine need for us. As a race and as individuals, we have a vocation.

A key ingredient of the tragic vision of life is an exquisite awareness of life's brevity conjoined to the conviction that this life is the only one. After King Lear's daughter is killed because of his pride and foolishness, Lear comes on stage bearing Cordelia's corpse and crying:

> Howl, howl, howl, howl! O, you are men of stone.
> Had I your tongues and eyes, I'd use them so
> That heaven's vault should crack. She's gone for ever! . . .
> No, no, no life!
> Why should a dog, a horse, a rat, have life,
> And thou no breath at all? Thou'lt come no more,
> Never, never, never, never, never![13]

Surely all bereaved parents have shared Lear's grief and wished to crack the vault of heaven with their protest. But just as surely, the real tragedy of Lear's grief lies not in his loss itself but in that terrible five-fold "Never!" If the "never" is true we can repair for no greater wisdom about life than to Shakespeare and the Greek tragedians.

St. Paul agrees:

> If there be no resurrection, then Christ was not raised; and if Christ was not raised, then our gospel is null and

void, and so is your faith . . . . It follows also that those who have died in Christ's fellowship are utterly lost. If it is for this life only that Christ has given us hope, we of all men are most to be pitied. But the truth is, Christ was raised to life—the first fruits of the harvest of the dead . . . .—Christ the first fruits, and afterwards, at his coming, those who belong to Christ (I Cor. 15:13–14, 18–20, 23).

So Christians respectfully disagree with Lear. Respectfully, because we do not wish in any way to denigrate his grief nor the preciousness of human life. We must part company with him with respect, with hope, with faith and with great conviction. For we believe that the God who had the power to fill darkness with light at the creation, has power to fill the dead with new life at the resurrection.

We believe in the power of God. And, even more, we believe in the love of God. The Christian story is not a tragedy but a romance. So, most emphatically, we part company with Lear's theology. He said: "As flies to wanton boys are we to the gods—they kill us for the sport."[14] Because of what God has done for us in Christ, and because of what he has revealed himself to be in Christ, we have a very different image of God. We know him as the Good Shepherd: "I am the good shepherd; I know my own sheep and my sheep know me—as the Father knows me and I know the Father—and I lay down my life for the sheep. But there are other sheep of mine not belonging to this fold, whom I must bring in; and they too will listen to my voice. There will then be one flock, one shepherd" (Jn. 10:14–16).

But how about all the sheep purloined from the shepherd's flock? God said, "Thou shalt do no murder" (Ex. 20:13 KJV). But wicked men murder every hour. Their victims' deaths are clearly contrary to God's will. A clear theme of Scripture is God's attempt to teach us wisdom; yet, people are killed by foolishness every day. Jesus refuted those who thought sickness a visitation of God (cf. Jn. 9:1–3); disease is an enemy of God; that is what all the healing miracles were about. What are we to say then about all the premature deaths from disease?

Does God simply lose the fight sometimes? It would seem so. People are killed in accidents, many caused by drunken drivers. Men and women waste away ravaged by cancer. Devout Christians are slaughtered the world over. Many were murdered by Idi Amin and his Muslim henchmen. Nuns were murdered by leftist guerrillas in Zimbabwe. Priests were stretched on the rack by a rightist junta in Brazil. And they are just the last in a long red line. St. Paul quotes the Psalmist of himself: "for your sake we are killed all the day long; we are accounted as sheep for the slaughter" (Rom. 8:36, cf. Ps. 44:22). Jesus himself was led like a lamb to the slaughter.

With what sorrow, anger and frustration God must watch over us, like a mother's stricken vigil at the bedside of a child in pain. Is this indeed the way life is—God the loving shepherd watching over his sheep as best he can but losing some to the forces of evil?

I could accept that. It would be enough for me to know that God, like my human father, loved me and cared what happened to me and was on my side. I would not expect him to keep all his sheep safe in the flock. I could be content with his losing a few.

But Christ is not content.

Christ will not accept the loss of a single sheep: "My own sheep listen to my voice; I know them and they follow me. I give them eternal life and they shall never perish; no one shall snatch them out of my hand" (Jn. 10:17–28).

No one. Not cancer, not foolishness, not Hitler, not Amin, not guerrillas or tyrants, not the devil himself. No one.

> Who shall separate us from the love of Christ? Shall tribulation, or distress, or persecution, or famine, or nakedness, or peril, or sword? . . . No, in all these things we are more than conquerors through him who loved us. For I am sure that neither death, nor life, nor angels, nor principalities, nor things present, nor things to come, nor powers, nor height, nor depth, nor anything else in all creation, will be able to separate us from the love of God in Christ Jesus our Lord (Rms. 8:35, 37–39).

But where then are the lost ones? They are not lost. Then where are they? Where are Christ's sheep? Why, they are with Christ, every one of them. Christ, the once slaughtered lamb, sits now upon the throne as shepherd, and his sheep surround him day and night:

> After this I looked and saw a vast throng, which no one could count, from every nation, from all tribes, peoples and languages standing in front of the throne and before the Lamb. They were robed in white and had palms in their hands, and they shouted together: "Victory

to our God who sits on the throne, and to the Lamb!" . . . .
Then one of the elders turned to me [and said] . . . "These
are the men who have passed through the great ordeal . . .
and he who sits on the throne will dwell with them. They
shall never again feel hunger or thirst, the sun shall not
beat on them or any scorching heat, because the Lamb
who is at the heart of the throne will be their shepherd
and will guide them to the springs of the water of life;
and God will wipe all tears from their eyes" (Rev. 7:9–10,
13–17).

A Song of Celebration

For all the saints, who from their labors rest,
Who thee by faith before the world confessed,
Thy name, O Jesus, be forever blessed.
Alleluia, alleluia!

Thou wast their rock, their fortress, and their might:
Thou, Lord, their Captain in the well fought fight;
Thou, in the darkness drear, the one true Light.
Alleluia, alleluia!

O blest communion, fellowship divine!
We feebly struggle, they in glory shine;
Yet all are one in thee, for all are thine.
Alleluia, alleluia!

And when the strife is fierce, the warfare long,
Steals on the ear the distant triumph song,
And hearts are brave again, and arms are strong.
Alleluia, alleluia!

But lo! there breaks a yet more glorious day;
The saints triumphant rise in bright array;
The King of glory passes on his way.
Alleluia, alleluia!

From earth's wide bounds, from ocean's farthest coast,
Through gates of pearl streams in the countless host,
Singing to Father, Son and Holy Ghost,
Alleluia, alleluia![15]

AMEN

Notes

Biblical quotations are from the New English Bible (NEB) unless otherwise noted. Other versions quoted are the King James Version (KJV), the Jerusalem Bible (JB) and the Revised Standard Version (RSV).

PREFACE

[1] Richard Hooker. See *Lesser Fasts and Feasts*. The Church Hymnal Corp., NY: 1980. Page 367.

CHAPTER 1: KNOWLEDGE

[1] Sir Isaac Newton in letter to Robert Hooke, 1676. See J. Weaver. *The World of Physics*. Simon & Schuster, NY: 1987. Vol. I, Page 482.

[2] See Sir George Thomson. "What You Should Know About Physics" in *Adventures of the Mind*, 2nd Series. Vintage Books, NY :1961. Page 41.

[3] See William Paley. *Natural Theology*. Ch. 1. Cf. Voltaire, *Traite de Metaphysique* Chapter II: "When I see a watch whose hands mark the hours, I conclude that an intelligent being has arranged the springs of this machine so that its hands will mark the hours. Thus, when I see the springs of the human body, I conclude that an intelligent being has arranged these organs to be received and nourished for nine months in the womb; that the eyes are given to see, the hands to grasp, etc."

[4] Walt Whitman. *Leaves of Grass*, "Song of Myself," line 31.

[5] Peter Robinson. "Faith and Reason" in the *Wall Street Journal*, June 12, 1988. Page W13.

[6] In Kant's terms, we can perceive only the phenomenon not the noumenon, only the thing as it appears to us not the thing in itself. See Immanuel Kant. *Critique of Pure Reason*, Transcendental Analytic, Book II, Chapter III. *Kant Selections*. Charles Scribner's Sons, NY: 1929. Pages 145-155.

7   From the legends of Reynard, the fox, in Roman de Renart.

8   See Anselm. *Proslogion*. Chapters II-III., in *Saint Anselm, Basic Writings*. Open Court, LaSalle, Ill.: 1962. Page 8.

9   From the song "Smoke Gets in Your Eyes," by Jerome Kern.

10 "The Didache," *The Apostolic Fathers*. CIMA, NY: 1947. Pages 180-181.

11 Albert Einstein quoted by Stephen Hawking in *A Brief History of Time*. Bantam Books, NY: 1988. Page 56.

12 See "The Burial of the Dead: Rite One," *The Book of Common Prayer*. Oxford University Press, NY: 1979. Page 469.

13 LaPlace in 1799 on being asked by Napoleon where God was in his *Mercanique celeste, I*. See *A New Dictionary of Quotations on Historical Principles*. Edited by H. L. Mencken. Alfred Knopf, NY: 1976. Page 465b.

14 Cf. Blaise Pascal. *Pensess*. E. P. Dutton, NY: 1958. Page 72.

15 Rabindranath Tagore. *Gitanjale*. MacMillian and Co., Ltd., London: 1961. Page 34.

CHAPTER II. GOD

1   See Michio Kaku and Jennifer Trainer. *Beyond Einstein*. Bantam Books, NY: 1987.

2   Diotima to Socrates in Plato's *Symposium*.

3   See John Milton. *Paradise Lost*. Book VIII, lines 615ff.

4   Matthew Arnold. "Dover Beach," last two stanzas. *A Treasury of Great Poems*. Edited by Louis Untermeyer. Simon & Schuster, NY: 1955. Page 922.

5   See A. J. Ayer. *Language, Truth and Logic*. Dover Publications Inc., NY: 1946. Chapter VI, especially Page 107.

6   In Fyodor Dostoyevski's *Crime and Punishment*.

7   See Konrad Lorenz. *On Aggression*. Harcourt, Brace & World, NY: 1966.

8   See for example Desmond Morris's *The Naked Ape*. McGraw Hill, NY: 1967.

9   William Shakespeare. *Macbeth*. V, v, 19-28.

10 See Augustine. *De Trinitate*. V, 9.

11 John Macquarrie. *Principles of Christian Theology*, 2nd Edition. Charles Scribner's Sons, NY: 1977. Page 199.

[12]   Gregory of Nazianzus makes a similar analogy in "The Fifth
       Theological Oration," *Christology of the Later Fathers*.The
       Westminister Press, Philadelphia: 1954. Section 32, Page 213.
[13]   Hymn 516, verses 1 and 2, *The Hymnal*, 1982. The Church
       Hymnal Corp. Cooperstown, NY: 1985.
[14]   Cf. Augustine. Sermon 71 and *De quanitate animae* 34, 77.
[15]   Macquarrie. op. cit. Pages 198-199, 201
[16]   *The Book of Common Prayer*. Page 358.
[17]   See Thomas Aquinas. *De Ente et Essentia*, Chap. V and the
       Prima Secundae Q 37, Art. 1 & 2.
[18]   Quoted by Kallistos Ware. *The Orthodox Way*. St. Vladimir's
       Seminary Press, Crestwood, NY: 1980. Page 51.
[19]   *Ibid*. Page 57.
[20]   Theoklitos of Dionysiou. Quoted by Ware. *Ibid*. Page 52.

CHAPTER III: CREATION

[1]   Macquarrie. op. cit. Page vii.
[2]   I am speaking of the God-made atoms. There are some additional
       man-made ones, but they exist for less than a second; they are
       not the stuff of which solid reality is made.
[3]   Gary Zukav. *The Dancing Wu Li Masters*. Bantam Books,
       NY:1979. Page 208.
[4]   *The Restless Universe*. Dover, NY: 1951. Page 206.
[5]   *San Antonio Light*, Jan. 28, 1983. Page 5C.
[6]   Alan Lightman. "One Stuff" in *Harvard Magazine*, July-August
       1999. Page 27. A fuller discussion of advances in physics since
       the 1950's, written for laymen, may be found in Brian Greene's
       The Elegant Universe. W.W. Norton & Co., NY: 1999. Pages
       3-20 summarize these developments.
[7]   Shakespeare. *Richard III*, I, i, 18-21 and *Henry VI, Part III*, iii, 153-161.
[8]   Paul Coke, Episcopal Theological Seminary of the Southwest.
[9]   Cf. Job, Chs. 38-41.
[10]   Wesley is quoted to this effect by William Barclay. *The Gospel
       of Luke*. Westminster Press, Philadelphia: 1975. Page 164.
[11]   Cf. Paul Tillich. *Dynamics of Faith*. Harper Torchbook, NY:1958, Ch. III.
[12]   J.H. Shorthouse. *John Inglesant*. Macmillan Co., NY: 1900.
       Pages 40-41.

[13] "Song of the Three Young Men" verses 35-65, in *The Book of Common Prayer*. Pages 88ff.

CHAPTER IV: MAN

[1] Protagoras in Plato's *Theaetetus*.

[2] Cf. op. cit.

[3] Quoted by Abraham Heschel. *Who Is Man?* Stanford University Press, Stanford: 1965. Page 24.

[4] See Plato. *Meno*.

[5] Shakespeare, *The Tempest*. V, i, 148-158.

[6] Augustine. *Confessions*. I, 1. Sheed & Ward, NY: 1942. Page 3.

[7] In the words of Karl Rahner, contemporary Roman Catholic theologian.

[8] See Sophocles. *Oedipus Rex*.

[9] See Martin Luther. *On the Bondage of the Will*. Chap. II, viii. James Clark & Co. Ltd., London:1957. Pages 103-104.

[10] See John Calvin. *Institutes of the Christian Religion*, III, 21.

[11] Thomas Jefferson, First Inaugural Address, 4 March 1801, in *The Inaugural Addresses of the Presidents*. Edited by Jon Gabriel Hunt. Gramercy Books, NY: 1995. Page 25.

[12] Phillips Brooks. "Standing Before God" in *Selected Sermons*. Books for Libraries Press, Freeport, NY: 1949. Page 370.

[13] Percy Bysshe Shelley. "Ozymandias," *The New Oxford Book of English Verse*, 1250-1950. Edited by Helen Gardner. Oxford University Press. Oxford and NY: 1972. Page 580

[14] See D. H. Lawrence. "The Mosquito Knows" in *Selected Poems* The Viking Press, NY: 1967. Page 108.

[15] Winston S. Churchill. "Their Finest Hour," speech in the House of Commons, June, 18 1940, in *Churchill Speaks*, 1897-1963. Edited by Robert Rhodes James, M.P. Barnes & Noble, Inc., NY: 1980. Page 720.

[16] See Romans 5:12.

[17] See Augustine. *City of God* especially XIII, XIV.

[18] See Calvin. *Institutes*, II, 5.

[19] See L. S. B. Leakey "The Origin of the Genus Homo" in *Evolution After Darwin*, Vol. II. *The Evolution of Man*. University of Chicago Press, Chicago: 1960.

20   Nicolas Berdyaev. *The Divine and the Human*. Geoffrey Bles, London: 1949. Page 111.
21   In "Philosophy of Judaism" course, Union Theological Seminary. (Philosophy of Religion 205) November 3, 1965.
22   Cf. Ps. 104:19.
23   John Gossip. "Exposition of John" *Interpreter's Bible*. Abingdon Press, Nashville: 1952. Volume VIII, Page 510.

CHAPTER V: CHRIST

1   Plato. *Symposium*.
2   Richard Hooker. *Laws of Ecclesiastical Polity*, V, 56, 10.
3   Cf. Heschel. *Who Is Man?* Page 65.
4   Augustine. *Confessions*. I, 1. Page 3.
5   Cf. John 1:1-14.
6   Gregory of Nazianzus. "The Third Theological Oration On the Son" in *Christology of the Later Fathers*. Pages 173-175.
7   *The Book of Common Prayer*. Page 308.
8   Cf. *New York Times*, August 3, 1999 page A 6: "An analysis of pollen grains and plant images taken from the Shroud of Turin, believed by many Christians to be the burial shroud of Jesus, places the cloth's origin in or near Jerusalem before the eighth century . . . . Avinoam Danin, a botanist at the Hebrew University in Jerusalem, said at a news conference at the 16th International Botanical Congress [in St. Louis] . . . that analysis . . . identified them as coming from species that could be found only in the months of March and April in the Jerusalem region."
9   Cf. Hugh Joseph Schonfield. *The Passover Plot*. B. Geis Associates, distributed by Random House, New York: 1965.
10   Handel's *Messiah*.

CHAPTER VI: CHURCH

1   *The Book of Common Prayer*. Page 450.
2   Cf. *Doctrine in the Church of England*. Society for Promoting Christian Knowledge, London:1938. Appendix III, Page 224.

[3]   Lord Herbert quoted in Leslie D. Weatherhead. *In Quest of a Kingdom.* Abingdon-Cokesbury Press, Nashville: 1944. Page 210.

[4]   The last two sentences are a paraphrase of Macauley's essay on L. von Ranke's *History of the Popes.* Cf. Hans Kung. *The Church.* Sheed & Ward, NY: 1967. Pages 24-25.

[5]   *The Book of Common Prayer.* Pages 370-371.

[6]   Hymn 539 verse 2 in *The Hymnal* 1982. The Church Hymnal Corp., Cooperstown, NY: 1985.

[7]   *The Book of Common Prayer.* Page 308.

[8]   *Ibid.* Page 302.

[9]   *Ibid.* Page 303.

[10] *Ibid.* Page 427.

[11] *Ibid.* Page 160.

[12] See *Ibid.* Page 450. Cf. Lk.15:11-21.

[13] Teresa of Avila. *The Interior Castle.*

[14] Matthew Fox, O.P. *Meditations with Meister Eckhart.* Bear & Co., Inc., Santa Fe, NM: 1982. Page 82.

[15] L. Lamont. *Day of Trinity.* New American Library, NY: 1965. Page 180.

[16] *Ibid.*

[17] Arnold Toynbee. Unpublished notes by a member of the audience of a speech at the University of Pennsylvania, 1961.

[18] First Inaugural, March 4, 1801. in Hunt, ed., *Inaugural Addresses.* Page 26.

[19] Seventh Lincoln-Douglas Debate, Alton, Illinois on October 15, 1858. *Abraham Lincoln: Speeches and Writings.* The Library of America, NY: 1989. Volume I, Page 811.

CHAPTER VII: HOPE

[1]   Shakespeare, *The Tempest.* IV, i, 152-154, 156.

[2]   Cf Jesse Greenstein. "Natural History of a Star" in *Adventures of the Mind.* 2nd Series. Page 246.

[3]   Robert Frost. "Fire and Ice" in *Complete Poems of Robert Frost.* Holt, Rinehart and Winston, NY: 1964. Page 268.

[4]   Cf. Mk 4:35-41.

[5]   John Donne. "Holy Sonnet VII" in *The Poems of John Donne.* Oxford University Press, London: 1960. Page 296.

6   George Every. *The Time of the Spirit*. St. Vladimir's Seminary
    Press, Crestwood, NY: 1984. Page 166.
7   Shakespeare. *Hamlet*. III, i, 79-80.
8   Raymond A. Moody. *Life After Life*. Stackpole. Mechanicsburg,
    PA: 1975.
9   For the meaning of "miracle" see Page 117.
10 Elie Wiesel. *Night*. Discus Books, NY: 1958. Pages 42, 44.
11 *Hamlet*. III, i, 79-80.
12 *Macbeth*, V, v, 26ff.
13 Shakespeare, *King Lear*. V, iii, 258-259, 304-308.
14 *Ibid*. IV, i, 36.
15 Hymn 287 verses 1-2, 4-5, 7-8 in *The Hymnal* 1982.

Index to Biblical References

Genesis
1: 1–2, 72; **1f**, 63; **4**, 77; **10**, 77 ; **12**, 77; **18**, 77; **21**, 77; **25**, 77; **26–27**, 56, 95; **26–30**, 89; **27**, 98; **31**, 77
3: **4f**, 139; **5**, 139

Exodus
16: **10**, 210
20: **2–17**, 102; **3**, 213; **4**, 55; **13**, 228
22: **21–27**, 79
33: **18**, 210; **22**, 210
34: **29**, 210
40: **34**, 210

Deuteronomy
30: **11–15**, 104

I Samuel
15: **2–3**, 26

Job
3: **15**, 31

Psalms
8: **4**, 89
24: **1–2**, 83
33: **15f**, 91
42: **7**, 62
44: **22**, 228
49: **10–11**, 82
50: **14**, 179
55: **19**, 106
76: **12**, 107
90: **10**, 90
94: **9**, 55
95: **4–5**, 83
96: **8**, 179
100: **3**, 83
104: **5**, 59; **6–9**, 72; **10–22**, 59; **19**, 236n22; **28–31**, 59
139: **7–8**, 209

Isaiah
1: **2–3**, 113

Jeremiah
2: **13**, 103

Hosea

6:     **6,** 123

Amos

5:     **8,** 207

8:     **4,** 106

Ecclesiasticus

2:     **18,** 114

15:    **16f,** 220

Chap. **43,** 114

Matthew

1:     **20,** 171

3:     **9,** 218; **12,** 220

4:     **1–11,** 139; **4,** 139; **7,**
       139; **10,** 139

5:     **6,** 104; **19,** 123; **20,**
       123; **21ff,** 123; **23f,**
       136; **27f,** 123; **33f,**
       123; **38f,** 123; **43–48,**
       134, 112; **44,** 136;
       44–45, 97; **48,** 139

6:     **2ff,** 145; **5–9,** 136;
       7–9, 126; **12,** 135;
       14-15, 135; **16,** 145;
       19f, 131; **24,** 131; **27,**
       141; **31–33,** 132

7:     **9–11,** 132; **15,** 140; **21,**
       215

9:     **13,** 123; **22,** 141; **27,**
       141; **29,** 141

12:    **1–14,** 142; **7,** 123, 136

13:    **44–46,** 132; **54ff,** 152

14:    **23,** 136

15:    **7,** 145; **21–28,** 153; **22,**
       139; **26,** 119; **28,** 141

16:    **28,** 100

17:    **15,** 139

18:    **1–6,** 222; **2–4,** 156; **8,**
       222; **8–9,** 219; **10,** 222;
       23, 135; **23ff,** 188;
       23–35, 135

19:    **13,** 136

20:    **1–15,** 124; **25ff,** 147;
       25–28, 220; **30,** 141

21:    **28–31,** 216

22:    **18,** 145; **20,** 198; **21,**
       198; **36–40,** 133

23:    **13,** 145

24:    **2,** 204; **19–21,** 206; **20,**
       136; **27,** 205; **29,** 205

Chap. **24,** 168

25:    **31–46,** 137, 195, 218

26:    **26–28,** 147; **33,** 32; **35,**
       32; **36,** 136, **41,** 136

27:   **5,** 186

28:   **11–15,** 156; **18f,** 182; **19,** 192

Mark

1:   **10–11,** 171; **13,** 152; **14f,** 122; **15,** 140, 187

2:   **1–12,** 188; **5ff,** 142; **10,** 155; **27,** 144, 120

5:   **34,** 141

6:   **35–44,** 146; **46,** 136

7:   **1–8,** 200; **8,** 123; **15,** 123

9:   **1,** 119; **35,** 200; **42–48,** 222; **43,** 219

10:   **4–5,** 124; **14,** 183; **15,** 167; **42ff,** 200; **47,** 141; **52,** 117

11:   **12,** 119; **26,** 135

12:   **17,** 152

13:   **18,** 136; **32,** 200

Chap 13, 168

14:   **8,** 170; **32,** 113; **38,** 136

15:   **16,** 100; **26,** 155; **29,** 154; **31f,** 154; **34,** 153, 154

Luke

1:   **35,** 171; **42,** 136

2:   **9,** 210

3:   **11,** 84; **17,** 220

5:   **31,** 106

6:   **12,** 136; **28,** 136

7:   **34,** 152; **36–50,** 143; **50,** 141

8:   **48,** 141

9:   **28,** 136; **46–48,** 220

10:   **2,** 136; **4,** 152; **25–37,** 111, 216; **28,** 133; **33,** 134; **33ff,** 174; **36–37,** 134

11:   **2,** 136; **4,** 135

12:   **20f,** 131; **32,** 124–125; **32–34,** 132

13:   **19,** 122; **21,** 122

15:   **1–7,** 145; **11–21n12,** 237n12; **11–32,** 131

17:   **13,** 141; **19,** 141; **38,** 141

18:   **1,** 136; **17,** 167; **42,** 141

21:   **18,** 170; **26,** 205; **28,** 206

Chap. 21, 168

22:   **19,** 170; **30,** 56

23:   **34,** 152; **39–43,** 200

24:   **14–16,** 170; **30–31,**
          184

John

1:   **1–4,** 217; **14,** 181; **16,**
          194; **16–19,** 132

3:   **16,** 160; **3,** 167, 183; **8,**
          168

4:   **20–21,** 159; **6,** 119;
          7–9, 159

6:   **27,** 109; **48–51,** 184;
          54–56, 184; **67,** 219

7:   **53–8:11,** 151

8:   **4–11,** 143

Chap. 9, 181

9:   **1–3,** 228

10:   **14–16,** 227; **17–28,** 229

11:   **25ff,** 31

13:   **34f,** 146, 174

14:   **1,** 26; **16–19,** 160; **31,**
          136; **6,** 31, 193, 213,
          216,

15:   **4,** 191; **5,** 190; **11–13,**
          147; **12,** 186

Chap. 17, 136

18:   **36,** 196; **37,** 151

19:   **5,** 153; **10,** 151; **10–11,**
          196; **28,** 119

20:   **9–22,** 158; **19,** 170; **23,**
          188; **26,** 170; **28,** 157

21:   **4–7,** 170

Acts

9:   **1–2,** 163

17:   **27f,** 19; **27,** 209

Romans

5:   **12–13,** 164

7:   **7–11,** 165; **21–24,** 113

8:   **3–4,** 167; **14–16,** 162;
          35, 229; **36,** 226;
          37–39, 229

12:   **1,** 179

I Corinthians

11:   **23f,** 184; **24,** 170

12:   **1,** 169; **12,** 172; **17,**
          173; **27,** 172; **31,** 169

13:   **4–8,** 175; **13,** 175;
          1–13, 169

15:   **8,** 167; **13–14,** 227;
          18–20, 227; **23,** 227;
          35–37, 189; **35–38,** 212;

40, 212; **42–44,** 212;
53–55, 212; **57,** 212

II Corinthians

4: **5,** 177

5: **19–21,** 166

8: **9,** 195

Galatians

4: **29,** 168

5: **22–23,** 169; **25,** 169

6: **8,** 169

Ephesians

1: **19–23,** 171

4: **4–6,** 172; **12–16,** 176;
32–5:1f, 174

Philippians

3: **4–6,** 163; **7–9,** 164; **8f,**
32

Colossians

1: **12–20,** 160

I Timothy

6: **7,** 210

Hebrews

1: **1–3,** 115

James

2: **14–17,** 194

5: **3–5,** 200

I St. John

1: **1–2,** 21

3: **17,** 84, 160; **18,** 194

4: **7,** 56; **7–9,** 192; **9,** 56;
20–21, 192

Revelation

4: **11,** 179

7: **9–10,** 230; **13–17,** 230

Index to Keywords

Abraham, 53, 116, 218

Agape, 42, 116

Arnold, Matthew, 41

Ascension, 171

Augustine, Saint, 49, 51, 99, 108,
110

Authority, 14–15, 20–21, 26–27,
122, 125, 142, 147, 148, 155,
171, 182, 196

Ayer, A. J., 43

Barabbas, 154

Belief, 14, 28–31, 64, 180, 214

Berdyaev, Nicolas, 111

Body of Christ, 170, 172–754,
180

Born, Max, 66

Brooks, Phillips, 104

Calvin, John, 100, 110

Chance, 16–18, 25, 57, 76, 138,
207

Christ, 20, 28, 31, 32, 92, 100,
115–158, 161, 162, 164,
166, 167, 169, 170–173,

174, 175–177, 178, 180–183,
184–185, 186, 187–188, 189,
190, 191, 192, 194, 195, 200,
201, 202, 203, 211, 212, 215,
214, 215, 216, 217, 218, 219,
224, 226–227, 229. *See also*
Jesus

Church, 20, 21, 27, 29, 48, 49,
53, 56, 64, 70, 73, 146, 157,
159–201, 202, 203, 213, 215,
217, 223

Churchill, Winston, 110

Compassion, 38, 54, 79, 84, 90,
116, 127, 128, 153, 158, 174,
216, 220, 222

Constantine, 196

Darwin, Charles, 78, 120

Decadence, 107–108

Demons, 140–141, 151

Devil, 100, 229

Discipleship, 32, 152, 169–170,
219

Domitian, 202

Dostoevsky, Fyodor, 43

Einstein, Albert, 16, 28, 66

Energy, 16, 49, 65–68, 73, 79, 85,
    86, 155, 170, 191, 212

Eros, 41, 108, 110, 115

Evolution, 45, 57, 63, 64, 76, 77,
    78, 79, 89, 96, 99, 111, 117

Experience, 12, 13, 18, 19, 20,
    21, 22, 23, 26, 28–29, 53, 54,
    55, 64, 78, 116, 129, 165,
    172, 173, 176, 187, 205, 208,
    209, 223

Faith, 4, 21, 22, 29–34, 41, 48,
    64, 78, 112, 119, 131, 139,
    141, 152, 153, 157, 158, 164,
    167, 172, 173, 175, 177, 181,
    188, 190, 191, 193, 194, 202,
    203, 214, 216, 217, 218, 219,
    221, 222, 224, 227, 231

Father, 39, 49–50, 51, 52–54, 55,
    56, 70, 88, 96, 118, 121, 124,
    125–130, 132, 135, 136, 137,
    142, 147, 148, 155, 158, 159,
    160, 162, 171, 172, 178, 180,
    181, 182, 183, 190, 205, 213,

    213, 214, 215, 216, 217, 218,
    219, 222, 227, 231

Finite, 43, 55, 74, 76, 91, 93, 99,
    101, 108

Finitude, 26, 36, 60, 74–78,
    89–91, 93, 97, 105

Force, 12, 42, 54, 55, 58, 68–71,
    77, 161, 185, 202

Forgiveness, 42, 131, 134–135,
    147, 148, 157, 174, 186–188,
    195, 222

Form, 63, 69, 71–72, 73, 74, 76

Fox, Matthew, 192

Francis, Saint, 43

Freedom, 52, 57, 60, 76, 99–101,
    111–113, 126, 127, 166, 185

Freud, Sigmund, 28, 117, 120

Galileo, Galilei, 73, 120

Generosity, 58, 80, 84, 124

Genghis Khan, 44

Glory, 48, 56, 61, 106, 121, 157,
    179, 180–181, 210, 212, 217,
    220, 223, 231

God, 11, 15, 18, 19, 20–22,
    24–27, 28–33, 34, 40–62, 63,
    64, 68, 70, 71, 72, 73, 74, 75,
    76, 77, 79, 80, 81, 82, 83,

84, 85, 86, 87, 89, 92, 93, 95,
96, 97, 98, 100, 102, 103,
106, 107, 108, 109, 110, 112,
113–114, 115–117, 118, 119,
120, 121, 122, 124, 125–126,
128, 129. 130, 132, 134,
135–137, 138–140, 141, 142,
143, 144, 147, 148, 149, 151,
152, 153, 154, 157, 158, 159,
160, 161, 162, 163, 164, 165,
166, 167, 168, 169, 171, 172,
173, 174, 175, 176, 177, 178,
179–180, 181, 183, 184, 185,
187, 189–190, 191, 192, 194,
195, 196, 198, 199, 201, 203,
204, 206, 207, 208, 209, 210,
212, 213, 214, 215–216, 217,
218–219, 221, 222, 223, 224,
226, 227, 228, 229, 230
Gospel, 21, 30, 122, 136, 163,
172, 203, 213, 226
Grace, 57, 61, 79–82, 86, 100,
116, 125, 130, 141, 160–163,
166–167, 169, 180, 181, 183,
185, 186, 187, 189, 191, 202,
207, 209, 214, 218
Gratitude, 52, 80–81, 82, 84, 94,
106

Gregory of Nazianzus, 121

Hannibal, 148–149
Heaven, 39, 52, 63, 72, 87, 95,
96, 103, 121, 123, 127, 128,
131, 132, 135, 144, 145, 167,
171, 175, 179, 180, 182, 184,
203, 205, 208–210, 214, 215,
216, 219, 221
Hell, 129, 188, 208–210, 212,
219
Herod Antipas, 120
Heschel, Abraham, 6, 112
Hitler, Adolf, 43, 44, 109, 120,
215, 220, 222, 229
Holy Spirit, 50–54, 56, 70,
71, 72, 88, 140, 155, 158,
160–162, 171, 172, 175, 178,
182, 183, 184, 185, 189, 190,
191, 201, 211, 217, 218, 224
Humility, 81, 92, 105, 139, 140
Hypocrisy, 144, 176

Idol, 31, 53, 86, 102, 103, 116,
190, 199
Intuition, 13, 18, 25, 51, 52

Jefferson, Thomas, 199

Jesus, 20, 21, 28, 30, 31, 32,
    43, 50, 54, 106, 119–121,
    122–126, 131–148, 151–158,
    162, 163, 167, 170, 171, 174,
    177, 181, 182, 184, 185, 187,
    188, 190, 191, 194, 195, 196,
    198, 202, 203, 204, 205, 206,
    201, 212, 213, 215, 216, 217,
    219, 221, 228, 229, 231,
    236n8. *See also* Christ
Job, 31, 33
John the Baptist, Saint, 122,
    219–220
John the Divine, Saint, 179,
    202–203
John, Saint, 56, 143, 211, 215
Judas Iscariot, 186–187
Justice, 43, 44, 45, 47, 84, 132,
    133–134, 136, 173, 190, 198,
    199–200
Justification, 124, 144, 164, 166

Khomeini, Ayatollah, 214
Knowledge, 11–39, 50, 70, 73,
    92, 95, 106, 113, 118, 168,
    186, 193

LaPlace, Pierre Simon, Marquis
    de, 34
Law, 12, 16, 17, 34, 50, 51–52,
    71, 72, 74, 77, 78, 84, 86, 94,
    102, 103, 106, 112–113, 122,
    123, 130, 132, 133–134, 135,
    137, 142, 143, 144, 145, 148,
    151, 163–168, 190, 198, 199,
    200–201, 207, 225
Limits, 22–28, 36, 47, 60, 72,
    74–77, 89–90, 92, 109, 124,
    133, 175
Lincoln, Abraham, 199
Logos, 50–51, 72, 72, 215
Lorenz, Konrad, 45
Love, 14, 37–39, 40, 41–43, 45,
    47, 51, 54, 56–57, 58, 61–62,
    64, 68–70, 77, 80, 81–82,
    84, 85, 86, 92, 96, 97, 98,
    99, 108, 114, 115, 116, 120,
    122–124, 126, 127, 129, 130,
    131, 132, 134, 135–136,
    137–138, 140, 141, 142–144,
    146, 147, 149, 151, 153, 155,
    158, 160, 161, 166, 168, 173,
    174–175, 176, 180, 181–182,
    183, 185, 186, 188, 189, 190,
    191, 192, 193, 194–195, 201,

202, 209, 216, 217, 218, 223, 225, 227, 229

Luke, Saint, 142

Luther, Martin, 100, 114

Macquarrie, John, 51

Magic, 29, 161, 181, 215, 219

Mark, Saint, 142

Mary, Saint, 117

Matter, 65–71, 72, 73, 74, 75, 77, 79, 85, 156, 170, 212

Meaning, 32, 43, 44, 45–47, 79–80, 84–85, 117, 118, 146–147, 163, 223

Mercy, 38, 42, 114, 116, 120, 123, 133–134, 136, 138, 140, 141, 142, 186, 188, 194–196, 200–201, 222

Milton, John, 41

Miracle, 17, 26, 141, 189, 211, 228

Money, 27, 91, 125, 126, 131, 163, 198

Moses, 20, 50, 53, 143, 210

Mystery, 15, 36, 48, 49, 53, 54, 67, 99, 121, 161, 168

Newton, Isaac, 12, 15, 28, 30

Oppression, 199

Paul, Saint, 110, 162–169, 174, 175, 177, 218, 226, 228

Perception, 11–12, 15, 22–23, 25, 81, 92, 105, 112, 116, 181, 223, 232n6

Peter, Saint, 31, 218

Pilate, Pontius, 148–156, 158 196, 202

Pity, 38, 134–135, 195, 224

Power, 18, 36, 37, 38, 42, 47, 51, 54, 57, 60–61, 74, 80, 86–88, 115, 120, 138, 139, 140, 141, 151, 154, 155, 156, 161, 162, 168, 169, 171, 172, 179, 180, 185, 188, 189, 196, 197, 198, 199, 201, 210, 211, 212, 227

Pride, 80, 81, 105–108, 128, 130, 166, 169, 226

Providential, 57–58

Reason, 12–13, 15–17, 20, 23–25, 30, 50, 51–52, 56, 103, 113, 118, 213

Resurrection, 31, 43, 128, 156,
    157, 158, 189, 211–212, 226,
    227
Revelation, 13, 14, 20, 25–26, 48,
    50, 56, 217
Righteousness, 54, 88, 103–105,
    106, 110, 122–123, 124, 129,
    131, 137, 144–145, 163, 164,
    167, 217, 218
Romance, 227

Sacraments, 84–85, 86, 177,
    180–189, 191
Samuel, 26
Satan, 138–140, 141, 185
Saul, 26
Self-righteous, 162, 164, 173
Sense, 11–12, 15, 22–23, 26, 47,
    91, 96, 100, 119
Shakespeare, William, 17, 71,
    97–98, 204, 224, 226
Sign, 84, 85, 99, 155, 181
Sin, 27, 41, 42, 54, 61, 81,
    105–108, 110–113, 115,
    119, 121, 127, 128, 129, 138,
    141, 142–143, 144, 145, 147,
    148, 151, 154, 155, 159, 161,
    164–165, 166, 167, 175, 176,

    177, 185, 187, 188, 195, 199,
    207
Socrates, 30, 94, 215
Son, 50–54, 56, 70, 72, 88, 115,
    125-131, 132, 140, 141, 142,
    147, 148, 157, 159, 162, 167,
    181, 182, 187, 194, 205, 216,
    217
Spirit, 14, 20, 27, 50–52, 56, 59,
    63, 65, 67, 68, 70, 71, 72, 73,
    85, 88, 95, 107, 108, 140,
    155, 158, 160–162, 166, 167,
    168–169, 170, 171, 172, 175,
    178, 180, 181, 182, 183, 184,
    185, 189, 190, 191, 199, 201,
    209, 211, 212, 217, 218, 224
Spirituality, 29, 85, 95–96, 97,
    99, 101, 103, 108, 113, 173,
    181, 190–192
Stewardship, 82–83
Substance, 13, 40, 52, 65–70,
    73–74
Symbol, 19, 55, 72, 85, 163, 181,
    225

Theoklitos of Dionysiou, 61
Thomas Aquinas, Saint, 56
Thomas, Saint, 157

Townes, Charles, 17

Tragedy, 225, 226, 227

Trinity, 47–54, 57, 70, 72, 98

Virtue, 92, 94, 97–101, 111, 148,
   152, 153, 166, 197

Wesley, John, 84

Wiesel, Elie, 221–222

Works, 58, 86, 107, 166, 173,
   194–195, 218